Why Women Love Men Who Can Cook

Love Matters in the
Kitchen and in
Women's Friendships.

NICCI BROCHARD
&
DR. BEN CHUBA

Why Women Love Men Who Can Cook

Love Matters in the
Kitchen and in
Women's Friendships.

CROSSBORDER

New York, London, Quebec

CONTENT

FORWARD

What an interesting time we have for you as you pick up this book. There's something undeniably seductive about a man who knows his way around a kitchen. Perhaps it's the confidence in his movements as he dices an onion with practiced precision, or the vulnerability displayed when he admits his soufflé has fallen. Maybe it's the intimate act of nourishment, creating something with his hands meant to sustain, comfort, and sometimes, impress.

This book began one evening in when we were at dinner, where eight women and 4 men gathered around our dining table. The conversation flowed as freely as the wine, and inevitably turned to relationships. Nene, newly engaged, recounted how her fiancé won her heart not with grand gestures, but with a simple homemade pasta on their third date. Around the table, heads nodded in recognition.

What emerged that night was a tapestry of stories confirming what many of us intuitively know: culinary skill in a partner represents something far deeper than mere utility. It speaks to attention, care, patience, and a willingness to nurture; qualities that resonate profoundly in romantic relationships and mirror what women often seek in their deepest friendships.

Nicci Brochard & Dr.Ben Chuba

With this book, we intend to explore this fascinating intersection of food, love, and connection, where the kitchen becomes both laboratory and stage for the heart's most essential work.

Nicci and I (Ben) want to thank you in advance for trusting us with your valuable time.

INTRODUCTION
Love, Friendship, and the Magic of a Good Meal

There's something undeniably attractive about a man who can cook. Not just the kind who can throw together a decent spaghetti or grill a steak, but the kind who understands the magic that happens when flavors dance, when a kitchen becomes a sanctuary, and when a shared meal becomes an act of care. Ask almost any woman, and you'll hear it: there's just something about a man who knows his way around a stove.

This book isn't just about cooking ; it's about connection. It's about the way food has a unique power to bring people together, heal emotional wounds, and deepen bonds. It's about how the act of preparing a meal, when done with intention, can say what words sometimes can't: I see you. I value you. I want to nourish you.

But there's more to this story. In the pages that follow, we'll explore not just romantic dynamics between women and the men who impress them with their culinary confidence, but also the deep, often unspoken friendships between women that are built around food; through brunch dates, kitchen wine nights, recipe swaps, and soul-baring chats over steaming mugs of tea.

This is a love letter to kitchens, to the ones where flirtation begins over a sizzling pan, and the ones where sisterhood deepens while cookies bake. We'll dive into personal stories, cultural insights, a sprinkle of science, and plenty of real-life reflections on why the kitchen matters more than we think in how we love and connect.

Whether you're a man looking to understand the irresistible appeal of culinary confidence, a woman nodding knowingly because you've fallen for it before, or someone simply curious about how food weaves its way into our relationships, we got you covered.

So, pull up a chair, pour yourself a glass of something warm (or bubbly), and let's dig into the delicious dish that this book is about.

CHAPTER 1

The Historical Perspective

From Hearth to Hashtags: The Evolution of Gender Roles in Cooking

The kitchen has always been more than a place where meals are made. It is a place of tradition, of care, and of power. Across centuries and continents, the kitchen has played host to countless stories; from whispered secrets to declarations of love, from intergenerational wisdom to acts of resistance. Central to all these stories is the person holding the spoon. Historically, that person has usually been a woman.

This chapter traces the evolution of gender roles in cooking, showing how deeply rooted these roles are in societal structures, cultural expectations, and historical necessity. It also explores how those roles have been challenged, reshaped, and reimagined in modern times. Understanding the history helps us appreciate why a man who chooses to cook today often resonates with women on a deeper level. It signals a break from the past, a shift toward emotional intimacy, shared responsibility, and conscious care.

The Origins: Cooking as Survival and Symbolism

In early human societies, cooking was an essential survival skill. The discovery of fire, and the resulting ability to cook food, is often cited as a pivotal moment in human evolution. Cooking made food safer, more digestible, and calorie-rich, allowing for brain growth and social development. From the beginning, cooking was communal. In hunter-gatherer societies, while men often hunted, women gathered and prepared food, developing a deep knowledge of local plants, herbs, and grains.

Yet, this division was not merely about biology or physical ability. It was about roles within a survival-based economy. Women's knowledge of food was powerful. They knew how to ferment, preserve, and transform raw ingredients into meals. Cooking was more than sustenance; it was an art, a science, and a spiritual practice. In Indigenous societies around the world, from the Americas to Africa to Asia, food preparation was imbued with meaning. Meals were often prepared as offerings, as medicine, or as a way to pass on traditions.

Despite the central role women played in early food culture, their contributions were rarely documented. Oral traditions, passed from mother to daughter, preserved recipes and techniques, but the names of these women have largely been lost to history. Meanwhile, as civilizations developed and literacy spread, the people who wrote about food were often men, and they wrote for male audiences.

Ancient Civilizations: Gender, Class, and Culinary Power

In ancient Egypt, women were responsible for bread-making and beer-brewing, two staples of daily life. Artifacts and murals depict women engaged in these tasks, underscoring their centrality to both domestic life and religious rituals. In ancient Greece and Rome, however, a divide began to emerge. In wealthier households, cooking was considered menial work, often done by slaves or lower-class women. Upper-class women were expected to supervise, not participate.

At the same time, the concept of the "professional chef" began to emerge. In Roman society, male cooks who served elite families were trained and highly skilled. These men sometimes slaves, sometimes freedmen, could gain status through their culinary prowess. The seeds of culinary prestige were being planted, but it was a male garden.

In contrast, in many African and Asian cultures, women continued to dominate the kitchen. In Yoruba, Ethiopian, Indian, and Southeast Asian communities, food preparation was a deeply gendered but also revered practice. Mothers and grandmothers were guardians of the culinary soul of the family. Their kitchens were not just domestic spaces but cultural institutions.

Medieval to Early Modern Era: Women's Work and Men's Recognition

In medieval Europe, food preparation remained largely in the hands of women, especially in peasant households. Women grew vegetables, milked cows, made cheese, baked bread, and prepared stews that would feed large families. Cooking was labor-intensive and constant, yet invisible in the cultural narrative.

In aristocratic homes and monasteries, male cooks managed the kitchens. These cooks were respected professionals, organizing feasts that displayed the wealth and status of their patrons. Again, public culinary praise was largely reserved for men.

During the Renaissance and Enlightenment periods, European cuisine began to codify. French gastronomy, in particular, became formalized through the writings of male chefs. Cooking transitioned from a necessary skill to an art form; but only when practiced by men in elite kitchens. Female labor remained uncelebrated.

Colonialism and the Global Kitchen

The expansion of European empires brought about not only political and economic domination but also the exportation of domestic ideologies. Colonized women were often forced into roles of domestic servitude, including cooking. In the Americas and the Caribbean, enslaved African women cooked for white families, combining traditional African techniques with available local ingredients. The result was the birth of entirely new culinary traditions, Creole, Cajun, soul food, that blended cultures under duress.

These women, though exploited, created legacies through food. Their recipes were acts of resistance and resilience. Yet, once again, history erased their names, while European male chefs wrote cookbooks and received acclaim for recipes rooted in the labor and creativity of women of color.

2The 19th Century: Domestic Ideals and the Cult of the Housewife

The Industrial Revolution changed family life dramatically. With men working in factories and offices, the home became a symbol of feminine virtue. The "cult of domesticity" emerged, idealizing women as wives and mothers who created moral, peaceful homes. Cooking was moralized. A good woman fed her family well; a bad woman neglected the hearth.

Magazines, cookbooks, and etiquette guides reinforced this image. Cooking was a woman's duty, and doing it well was a sign of virtue. Yet the recipes women followed were often written by men. Cooking schools for women taught efficiency, hygiene, and servitude, not creativity or autonomy.

Ironically, in professional settings, male chefs continued to dominate. Hotels, restaurants, and royal courts hired men to cook at the highest levels. The same society that expected women to cook at home barred them from doing so professionally.

The World Wars: Shifting Roles and Wartime Kitchens

The World Wars forced a temporary but profound reimagining of gender roles. As men were drafted into service, women entered the workforce in unprecedented numbers. They also became heads of households, managing rations, growing victory gardens, and cooking creatively with limited supplies.

Government propaganda praised women for their resourcefulness. Cooking, once a taken-for-granted duty, became a patriotic act. Women shared tips, recipes, and support in community kitchens and through wartime pamphlets.

After the wars, many women were expected to return to domestic roles. The 1950s housewife was born: perfect hair, lipstick, and a meatloaf in the oven. Cooking regained its place as a symbol of femininity, but it was now wrapped in consumerism. New appliances, processed foods, and kitchen gadgets promised efficiency and happiness. Yet, for many women, it was a gilded cage.

The Feminist Movement and the Culinary Rebellion

By the 1960s and 70s, second-wave feminism began challenging the idea that a woman's place was in the kitchen. Women fought for equal pay, legal rights, and educational access. Some rejected cooking altogether, associating it with subjugation.

At the same time, others reclaimed cooking as an act of empowerment. Feminist writers and chefs began celebrating food as a source of creativity and independence. Community cookbooks, women-led co-ops, and alternative food movements flourished. The idea was simple: cooking should be a choice, not a chore.

Meanwhile, the rise of television cooking shows and food media launched male chefs into stardom. Julia Child broke barriers, but her male counterparts often received more recognition. Once again, when cooking became prestigious, men were invited back in with applause.

Contemporary Shifts: The Kitchen as a Shared Space

In the 21st century, gender roles in cooking are evolving rapidly. Men who cook are no longer outliers; they are often admired. Cooking is seen as a mark of independence, creativity, and emotional maturity. In dating culture, a man who can cook is seen as attractive not just because of the food, but because of what it represents: nurturing, thoughtfulness, and the ability to care.

Social media has played a huge role in this shift. Platforms like Instagram, TikTok, and YouTube have given rise to male cooking influencers who share recipes, date-night meals, and family dinners. These men are often praised for doing what women have done for centuries, yet their visibility helps normalize shared responsibility.

Women, too, are reclaiming cooking in new ways. Food blogging, home-based catering, and content creation allow women to profit from culinary skills once undervalued. The rise of wellness culture, ancestral cooking, and slow food movements has brought women back to the kitchen; not as servants, but as healers, historians, and entrepreneurs.

Why This History Matters

Understanding the evolution of gender roles in cooking helps us recognize the significance of today's dynamics. When a man cooks now, he is participating in a legacy that women have carried, often silently for millennia. He is stepping into a space shaped by labor, love, and care. And when he does so with humility and intention, it is deeply attractive.

It tells a woman: I see the value in what you do. I want to contribute. I want to care.

Likewise, women's friendships, so often centered around food, reflect centuries of shared stories, recipes, and rituals. Cooking together, eating together, feeding each other; these are not just acts of nourishment, but of bonding.

As we move forward, the kitchen is becoming a more inclusive, equitable, and joyful place. And in that space, love, whether romantic or platonic can flourish.

CHAPTER 2

Culinary Skills as an Attractive Trait

In modern romantic dynamics, societal roles and expectations have undergone a significant transformation. Among the myriad traits that women seek in romantic partners, culinary skill has steadily risen to become one of the most admired. A man who knows his way around the kitchen, not only by boiling pasta or scrambling eggs, but by cooking with flair, creativity, and attention to detail, often finds himself more favorably positioned in the dating landscape.

This chapter explores the allure of culinary competence in men through the lens of academic research, social surveys, and insights from leading relationship experts. It dissects why the ability to cook holds psychological, emotional, and symbolic significance for many women, transforming it from a basic life skill into a powerful expression of affection, capability, and partnership.

Cooking as an Indicator of Emotional Intelligence and Self-Sufficiency

In an era that champions emotional intelligence and self-awareness as crucial traits for successful relationships, cooking offers a subtle but strong indicator of these attributes. A man who cooks not only demonstrates his ability to care for himself but also reveals his capacity to nurture others.

Dr. Alexandra Solomon, a clinical psychologist at Northwestern University and author of *Loving Bravely*, often refers to cooking as a "relational practice"—a tangible way of expressing empathy, foresight, and care. She emphasizes that when men cook for their partners, it reflects a form of emotional labor that women have historically shouldered. By stepping into the kitchen, men signal a willingness to participate in domestic and emotional responsibilities—a highly attractive quality in long-term partnerships.

In practical terms, a man preparing a meal—knowing his partner's favorite dish, shopping for the ingredients, preparing the meal attentively, and serving it with pride—encapsulates thoughtfulness in action. It is far more than sustenance; it is a love language, as meaningful as words of affirmation or acts of service.

What the Data Says: Studies and Surveys on Cooking and Attraction

The appeal of cooking isn't anecdotal; it's supported by a growing body of research. Numerous studies and surveys across different cultures reveal that women consistently rank culinary ability as a desirable trait in romantic partners.

1.   The Elite Singles Survey (2018)

A comprehensive study by Elite Singles, a popular online dating platform, revealed that nearly 86% of women rated cooking as the most attractive skill a partner could have. This placed cooking ahead of other traditionally valued traits such as financial stability, physical appearance, and career success. More than 30% of women even stated that they would prefer a partner who could cook over one who could offer luxury experiences such as exotic vacations or expensive gifts.

2.   The Psychology of Food and Behavior (University of Michigan)

A 2021 study from the University of Michigan's Department of Psychology examined the link between perceived nurturing traits and attractiveness. It concluded that women were more likely to associate men who cook with qualities such as patience, dependability, and a cooperative spirit. The researchers noted that women found men who could prepare a decent meal more "marriage-material" than those who could not.

3.   The British Heart Foundation Survey (2015)

This UK-based study found that women ranked cooking as the most romantic thing a partner could do for them, above writing love letters or planning surprise dates. The implication was clear: cooking, when done thoughtfully, can be one of the most direct ways to a woman's heart—not merely through her stomach, but through her emotional core.

4.   The "Man vs. Meal" Report by Tinder (2022)

Even in app-based, fast-paced dating culture, the trend holds. Tinder released a "Man vs. Meal" report showing that men who included cooking or food-related hobbies in their profiles received 26% more right-swipes from women. The platform also found that pictures of men cooking in their profiles led to longer conversations and more engagement.

The Symbolism of Cooking: What It Represents in Romantic Dynamics

Cooking is deeply symbolic. It signifies competence, stability, and attentiveness. For centuries, cooking has been culturally associated with nurturing—an inherently feminine-coded act. When a man cooks, especially in intimate or domestic settings, he disrupts traditional gender norms and enters a space of emotional parity.

Dr. Helen Fisher, a biological anthropologist at the Kinsey Institute, explains that women are biologically and socially primed to look for signals of partnership readiness. Cooking serves as one such signal—it showcases foresight, provision, and the ability to care not only for oneself but for others. It also subtly communicates humility and lack of entitlement: "I'm not waiting to be served; I can serve, too."

In relationships where domestic labor is more equally shared, satisfaction and longevity are statistically higher. A man who cooks often scores higher on scales of perceived partner value because he actively participates in sustaining the couple's well-being—not just financially or emotionally, but practically.

Relationship Experts on the Culinary Advantage

The consensus among relationship experts is almost unanimous: men who cook hold a distinct advantage in the dating and relationship space.

Esther Perel, Psychotherapist and Relationship Author

Perel, the globally renowned author of *Mating in Captivity*, has frequently spoken about the power of novelty and intentionality in long-term relationships. She identifies cooking as one of the most intimate forms of daily ritual that partners can share. In her podcast *Where Should We Begin?*, Perel recounts multiple client stories where the act of a husband preparing dinner rejuvenated a struggling marriage, reigniting affection, and admiration.

Gary Chapman, Author of The Five Love Languages

Chapman's framework emphasizes how love is best expressed in the preferred 'language' of a partner. Cooking often blends multiple languages: acts of service, quality time, and even physical touch (during shared preparation). Chapman has stated in interviews that men who learn to cook often discover it to be one of the most consistent and rewarding ways to express love.

Matthew Hussey, Relationship Coach

Hussey, known for his practical dating advice for women, encourages women to seek men who cook not merely for the convenience, but for the mindset it represents. In his masterclasses, he notes, "A man who cooks is a man who plans, who cares, who creates. These are the foundations of a lasting relationship."

Real-Life Examples That Speak Volumes

To understand how this plays out in real life, we can turn to stories of couples and individuals who have found cooking to be a transformative factor in their relationships.

Marcus and Elena – The Soup That Sealed the Deal

Elena, a project manager from Boston, shared how a simple meal turned into a defining moment in her relationship with

Marcus, a software developer. "We'd only been dating for about a month when I got the flu. He showed up with groceries, made chicken soup from scratch, and stayed to make sure I was okay. It wasn't just about the food, it was that he *knew* what would comfort me, and he did it without expecting anything in return." Elena later admitted that this moment made her realize she could see a future with Marcus. They're now engaged.

Sean – The Single Dad Who Cooked His Way Into A New Chapter

Sean, a single father of two from San Diego, used cooking as a bridge to reconnect with his children and navigate a new romantic relationship. "When I started dating again, I made it a point to cook for my dates. It showed them I could take care of myself and my kids. One woman told me it was the first time she ever felt truly 'seen' on a date not just taken out, but *cared for*." His culinary approach became his signature move, and eventually led to a serious relationship with his now-partner, Julia, a nurse, and fellow foodie.

The Evolution of Masculinity and Culinary Confidence

Cooking has become a cultural frontier for evolving masculinity. In generations past, men were rarely encouraged to enter the kitchen except to eat. Today, however, culinary confidence in men is not only accepted—it's celebrated. Cooking shows like *MasterChef, Chef's Table*, and *Salt Fat Acid Heat* have turned chefs into celebrities, and more men are embracing cooking as both an art form and a mode of expression.

There's also a rise in male-centric cooking communities online—from Reddit threads like r/CookingForMen to Instagram accounts where men share their kitchen creations with pride. This is more than a hobby; it's a shift in cultural identity.

Men like Action Bronson, David Chang, and even celebrities like Stanley Tucci and Idris Elba (who has shared his love for cooking in interviews) are redefining what it means to be a modern man: someone who can be strong and nurturing, driven, and domestic.

The Neuroscience of Attraction and Food

Scientific research suggests that food and attraction are neurologically linked. Cooking stimulates sensory pleasure—aroma, texture, and taste—activating the brain's reward centers. Sharing a meal, especially one that is homemade, creates a space for intimacy and vulnerability, both of which are precursors to emotional connection.

A 2019 study published in *Appetite* journal showed that participants who cooked together experienced higher oxytocin levels (the "bonding hormone") than those who simply dined together at restaurants. Cooking together, or for one another, literally makes couples feel more connected on a hormonal level.

Challenges and Opportunities: Not Every Man Starts as a Chef

One might argue that not every man is born with culinary talent. But that misses the point. What makes cooking attractive is not perfection, but intention. Women do not expect Michelin-level meals; they desire the presence of care, thought, and effort.

Men who start with small steps, learning how to make coffee the way she likes it, mastering breakfast, or crafting a simple date-night dinner, build confidence and skills over time. It becomes a growth journey that, when shared with a partner, becomes part of the relationship's unique story.

Conclusion
From Kitchen to Heart

Culinary skills, far from being a trivial bonus, are an embodiment of traits women value deeply in partners: thoughtfulness, competence, care, and emotional maturity. The act of cooking transcends gendered expectations and becomes a powerful tool for connection. Studies confirm it, relationship experts advocate for it, and real-life stories showcase its transformative impact.

As we continue to redefine romance and partnership in the modern age, it becomes increasingly clear: the man who can cook, who chooses to cook, and who shares that gift with his partner, holds a meaningful advantage, not because he flips the traditional script, but because he writes his own with intention, flavor, and love.

CHAPTER 3

Cooking and Emotional Connection

Food is more than just sustenance; it's a universal language that speaks to our senses, emotions, and relationships. Cooking, in particular, has the unique power to foster intimacy, strengthen bonds, and create lasting memories. The process of preparing food, sharing meals, and the communal experience of dining together are steeped in emotional significance. This chapter delves into how cooking fosters intimacy, explores the emotional impact of shared meals, and offers personal anecdotes that illustrate the profound connections formed around food.

How Preparing Food Fosters Intimacy and Strengthens Bonds

At its core, food is an expression of care and love. Preparing a meal for someone is an act of giving, whether it's a simple dish made with care, or a lavish spread created for a celebration. This gesture of preparing food for others is symbolic of nurturing, of providing something essential for the well-being of another person. The emotional connection fostered through cooking often transcends the act itself, creating bonds that are both personal and profound.

The Ritual of Cooking as a Form of Connection

The act of cooking together creates a space for connection and intimacy. When two or more people come together in the kitchen, the process of chopping vegetables, stirring pots, and seasoning dishes creates a shared experience that can't be replicated in other contexts. This shared time together is often filled with laughter, conversations, and even silence, as the act of cooking itself becomes a moment of comfort and unity. As a team, cooking involves cooperation and understanding, as people work together to achieve a common goal, the creation of a meal.

Cooking also provides an opportunity for individuals to express themselves, their cultures, and their histories. Food is deeply connected to identity, and when preparing a dish for someone else, there is often a sense of pride in sharing a piece of oneself through the food. For instance, a person might cook a family recipe passed down through generations, which adds a layer of history and tradition to the meal, deepening the emotional significance of the act.

Furthermore, food preparation often requires attentiveness and intention. It's not a task to be rushed or done mindlessly. When one takes the time to prepare food with care, it conveys a message of love and respect for the person being served. This level of attentiveness in cooking strengthens the bond between the cook and the person being cooked for. A study by the *Journal of Social and Personal Relationships* found that acts of care, such as cooking, create feelings of closeness and affection, often leading to greater relationship satisfaction.

Food as a Language of Love and Affection

Cooking for someone is often considered a universal expression of affection. In romantic relationships, this act can be particularly significant. Think of the classic gesture of preparing a homemade dinner for a partner, a meal made with their favorite ingredients, a carefully selected bottle of wine, and perhaps a dessert to top it all off. The very act of preparing the meal can evoke feelings of warmth, consideration, and attentiveness.

In families, cooking fosters a similar bond. Parents cooking for their children, or even the act of children learning to cook with their parents, helps to create a shared understanding of care and love. These experiences are often a foundation for deeper emotional connections, as food rituals help nurture not only the body but also the emotional well-being of all involved. It is through shared family meals that family traditions are passed down, and bonds are formed that transcend generations.

The Power of Food in Celebrating Life's Milestones

Food is integral to the rituals and celebrations that mark significant life events. Birthdays, weddings, anniversaries, holidays, and other milestones are often celebrated with meals. These celebrations are made more meaningful when food is prepared and shared with loved ones. The act of cooking for special occasions conveys a sense of care, and the shared experience of eating together reinforces feelings of belonging and love.

Whether it's a simple dinner to celebrate a small personal victory or an elaborate feast to commemorate a major life event, food plays a pivotal role in marking these moments. The very process of preparing and sharing a meal on such occasions turns the act of eating into a ritual, steeped in meaning and emotional significance. It's not just about the food; it's about the people, the memories created, and the connections formed over the shared experience.

Personal Anecdotes Illustrating the Emotional Impact of Shared Meals

A Family Tradition: Sunday Dinners with My Grandmother

One of my most cherished memories growing up was the Sunday dinners my grandmother prepared. Every Sunday, without fail, we would gather at her house for a hearty meal. The kitchen would be filled with the aroma of roast chicken, mashed potatoes, and the unmistakable scent of her famous apple pie baking in the oven. I can still hear the clinking of silverware, the chatter of family members, and the laughter that filled the room as we all sat down at the table together.

But it wasn't just about the food, it was about the love that went into preparing each dish. My grandmother, with her wrinkled hands and gentle smile, would spend hours in the kitchen, making sure everything was perfect. Each meal she made felt like a labor of love, a gift she gave to her family. As a child, I didn't fully appreciate the time and effort she put into those meals, but as I grew older, I realized that cooking wasn't just about the end product. It was about the moments we shared, the stories we told, and the deep sense of connection we felt as a family sitting around the table together.

Those Sunday dinners were more than just a routine; they were the foundation of our family's emotional connection. They represented comfort, togetherness, and the deep bonds that held us together. To this day, when I cook a meal for my own family, I can still hear my grandmother's voice and feel the warmth of those shared moments. Her meals were an expression of love that transcended the act of cooking, they created a space for us to come together, to share our lives, and to strengthen our emotional connection.

Cooking for My Partner: A Gesture of Love

When I first started dating my partner, I wanted to show him how much I cared through something meaningful and personal. I decided to cook a dinner for him, a simple meal of pasta with homemade tomato sauce and garlic bread. The ingredients were simple, but I poured my heart into the meal. I spent hours in the kitchen, chopping vegetables, simmering the sauce, and perfecting the flavors.

When my partner arrived, he was immediately struck by the effort I had put into the meal. We sat down at the table together, and as we ate, we talked about our day, our dreams, and the little things that made us who we were. The meal itself wasn't extravagant, but it was meaningful. It was an expression of my care, an intimate moment where we shared not only food but a piece of ourselves.

Since then, cooking for my partner has become one of our favorite rituals. We cook together on weekends, experimenting with new recipes or revisiting old favorites. It's not just about the food; it's about the time we spend together, the joy of creating something with our own hands, and the bond that grows with each meal we share.

Cooking with My Mother: A Lesson in Tradition

One of the most significant ways that cooking has fostered intimacy in my life is through the experiences I've shared with my mother in the kitchen. Growing up, I would often stand on a stool beside her while she prepared our family meals. She would teach me how to measure ingredients, how to taste and adjust seasoning, and the importance of patience in cooking. But it wasn't just about the technical skills—it was about the time we spent together, the stories she shared, and the quiet moments of connection.

Over the years, cooking with my mother became a cherished ritual, one that we both looked forward to. Even as I grew older and moved out of the house, cooking together became a way for us to reconnect, share our lives, and continue a family tradition that had been passed down through generations. The meals we created together weren't just about feeding the body—they were about nourishing our relationship and maintaining the emotional bonds that had been formed in the kitchen.

A Shared Meal at a Friend's House: The Power of Hospitality

In a more recent experience, I had the opportunity to visit a close friend's home for dinner. It wasn't a special occasion—just a casual evening where we decided to cook together and enjoy a meal. My friend had spent hours preparing a homemade dinner, and when I arrived, the house was filled with the delicious aromas of roasted vegetables and herbs. As we sat down to eat, there was an overwhelming sense of warmth and connection. The meal wasn't just food; it was a testament to my friend's generosity, care, and hospitality.

As we ate and shared stories, I realized that cooking together and sharing a meal created a unique bond between us. It wasn't about the quality of the food but the thoughtfulness behind it. The meal represented my friend's desire to nourish me, both physically and emotionally. It's moments like these that remind me of the profound impact that shared meals can have on relationships, how food can become a bridge that connects us to others in meaningful and unexpected ways.

Conclusion
The Emotional Power of Cooking and Shared Meals

Cooking is more than just a functional activity—it is a powerful means of creating emotional connections. From the simple act of preparing a meal for a loved one to the ritual of cooking together, food has a profound way of fostering intimacy and strengthening bonds. Whether it's a family tradition, a romantic gesture, or a shared meal with friends, the act of cooking and sharing food is an emotional experience that transcends the physical act of eating. Food, in this sense, becomes a language of love, care, and connection—one that speaks directly to the heart. The emotional impact of shared meals is immeasurable, and it's through these moments that we forge the strongest and most lasting bonds.

CHAPTER 4

The Psychology Behind Cooking Together

Cooking together as a couple is more than just preparing a meal; it's an opportunity to build connection, enhance communication, and strengthen the emotional bonds that underpin the relationship. In a world where fast-paced schedules, work commitments, and daily stresses can create emotional distance, engaging in shared activities like cooking offers a chance to reconnect, foster intimacy, and promote teamwork. This chapter explores the psychological dynamics of couples cooking as a team, as well as the benefits that collaborative meal preparation brings to relationship satisfaction.

Understanding the Dynamics of Couples Cooking as a Team

The Shared Experience of Cooking: A Foundation for Connection

Cooking together provides a shared experience where both partners actively engage in a task that requires cooperation, communication, and mutual respect. The kitchen becomes a space of collaboration, where each partner contributes to the creation of something meaningful: a meal that is nourishing both physically and emotionally. In contrast to other household chores that may feel mundane or obligatory, cooking together often feels like a creative and rewarding experience.

The dynamics between partners during this shared activity are unique. Unlike other tasks that might be done separately, such as cleaning or working, cooking requires joint effort. Whether it's chopping vegetables, stirring sauces, or setting the table, each step of the process involves communication and coordination. These interactions, even in their simplicity, encourage partners to work in tandem, reinforcing feelings of togetherness and mutual support.

Teamwork and Role Flexibility

Cooking as a couple fosters teamwork, where each person takes on specific roles but works together toward a common goal—the completion of a meal. These roles can be fluid, depending on the couple's preferences and the nature of the meal being prepared. In some cases, one partner might be the lead cook while the other assists with tasks such as setting the table, washing dishes, or preparing ingredients. Alternatively, both partners might share equal responsibility for every task, each bringing their strengths to the table.

Psychologically, the flexibility of roles in the kitchen is important. The ability to switch between tasks and adapt to each other's needs promotes a sense of equality and collaboration. It also allows couples to express their individual strengths— perhaps one partner excels at creating the main dish while the other shines in making a dessert or appetizer. This division of labor highlights the complementary nature of the relationship, with each partner contributing their unique skills.

Cooking together is also an excellent opportunity for couples to learn how to manage and resolve conflicts in a productive way. In the kitchen, things don't always go according to plan—burnt food, undercooked dishes, or a forgotten ingredient can quickly disrupt the flow. Navigating these challenges together requires patience, problem-solving, and a willingness to compromise. The ability to collaborate effectively in the kitchen, especially when things go wrong, can translate to improved conflict resolution in other areas of the relationship.

Physical Proximity and Nonverbal Communication

Cooking together also brings couples into physical proximity, which can create opportunities for nonverbal communication. Research in psychology has shown that physical closeness and touch are key components in building intimacy and emotional connection. When partners cook together, they are often physically close, passing ingredients, reaching for utensils, and moving around the kitchen as a team. These moments of shared space foster a sense of closeness and comfort.

Nonverbal cues, such as eye contact, smiles, or even simple gestures like handing over a dish or gently touching each other's hands, also enhance emotional bonding. These small but meaningful actions can communicate care, affection, and appreciation in a way that words sometimes cannot. For couples who may struggle with verbal communication, cooking together can serve as a powerful avenue for emotional expression, where the act itself conveys warmth and love.

Creativity and Shared Goals

The process of cooking together allows couples to express creativity and work toward a shared goal. Whether it's experimenting with a new recipe, modifying ingredients to suit personal tastes, or improvising when something unexpected happens, cooking becomes an exercise in creative collaboration. Creativity is a cornerstone of emotional connection; it allows individuals to bond over a shared sense of adventure and discovery.

Working toward the goal of creating a meal gives couples a sense of accomplishment. When the meal is prepared and shared, the feeling of achievement is mutual. This reinforces the idea that teamwork can lead to positive outcomes. The shared success of preparing a delicious meal also fosters positive emotions and satisfaction, which can contribute to a stronger, more resilient relationship.

Benefits of Collaborative Meal Preparation on Relationship Satisfaction

Strengthening Emotional Intimacy

Collaborative cooking enhances emotional intimacy by offering couples a chance to spend quality time together, free from distractions. The process of preparing a meal involves not only physical closeness but also emotional engagement. As couples work together, they create opportunities for shared conversations, laughter, and meaningful exchanges that contribute to a deeper emotional connection. These moments of closeness can help build trust and increase the sense of attachment between partners.

Emotional intimacy is fundamental to a successful relationship. By sharing tasks and engaging in meaningful, low-pressure activities like cooking, couples are able to enhance their emotional bond. In contrast to activities that may feel transactional or stressful, cooking together is often an enjoyable and relaxing experience that promotes positive feelings. As couples become more attuned to each other's needs and desires in the kitchen, they can apply these insights to other areas of their relationship, fostering a deeper sense of understanding.

Improved Communication Skills

Effective communication is one of the cornerstones of a successful relationship, and cooking together offers couples an opportunity to practice and improve their communication skills. Whether it's discussing the recipe, negotiating responsibilities, or offering feedback on the dish being prepared, cooking requires clear communication. Through this shared activity, couples learn how to articulate their thoughts, listen attentively to each other, and compromise when necessary.

In addition to verbal communication, couples also engage in nonverbal communication in the kitchen. Small gestures, like handing over an ingredient or sharing a smile, convey warmth and affection. The dynamic of working together in close quarters fosters a deeper understanding of each other's communication styles and strengthens the couple's ability to navigate future conversations, both trivial and serious.

Increased Relationship Satisfaction and Positive Reinforcement

The act of cooking together can positively impact overall relationship satisfaction. Engaging in joint activities that are pleasurable and productive creates positive reinforcement, which strengthens the emotional bond between partners. Shared experiences like cooking help couples create lasting memories and traditions that are tied to feelings of happiness and success.

Cooking also provides couples with the opportunity to practice gratitude. Whether it's expressing appreciation for the other person's efforts or simply acknowledging how well the meal turned out, cooking fosters a sense of mutual respect and recognition. Positive reinforcement of each other's contributions encourages feelings of appreciation and helps partners feel valued in the relationship. Over time, this can lead to greater relationship satisfaction and a deeper emotional connection.

Enhanced Collaboration and Problem-Solving

In any partnership, the ability to collaborate effectively and solve problems together is essential for long-term success. Cooking together fosters these skills by providing couples with opportunities to navigate challenges in a relaxed, low-stakes environment. Whether it's adapting a recipe to suit dietary preferences, managing time effectively to get everything on the table, or troubleshooting an unexpected culinary mishap, couples must work together to find solutions.

This type of collaborative problem-solving translates directly to other aspects of the relationship. Couples who can effectively navigate challenges in the kitchen are likely to apply the same teamwork and problem-solving skills to other areas of their lives, such as managing finances, making major life decisions, or resolving conflicts. The experience of working together in the kitchen reinforces the importance of cooperation, adaptability, and mutual respect in the relationship.

Boosted Physical Closeness and Touch

As previously mentioned, physical proximity in the kitchen naturally leads to more opportunities for touch and physical closeness. Touch is an important form of communication in relationships, and physical affection has been shown to reduce stress, increase happiness, and promote bonding. Cooking together often involves sharing small moments of touch, whether it's reaching over to grab a spoon or lightly brushing against each other as you move around the kitchen. These small physical gestures contribute to a sense of comfort and safety within the relationship, which in turn enhances emotional intimacy.

Creating Shared Memories

Finally, cooking together creates shared memories that couples can look back on with fondness. Whether it's a spontaneous meal cooked on a rainy day, or an elaborate dinner prepared for a special occasion, these memories become part of the couple's shared history. Over time, these experiences accumulate, strengthening the emotional foundation of the relationship. The act of cooking becomes a touchstone—a reminder of the joy, connection, and collaboration that defined those moments.

Conclusion
The Power of Cooking Together in Strengthening Relationships

Cooking together offers couples much more than just a way to prepare food—it's a powerful tool for enhancing emotional connection, communication, and collaboration. From fostering intimacy to improving problem-solving skills, the benefits of cooking as a team extend far beyond the kitchen. Through shared experiences, couples are able to create lasting memories, reinforce positive habits, and build stronger, more resilient relationships. In an increasingly busy and disconnected world, cooking together offers a simple yet profound way for couples to bond, reconnect, and cultivate the deep emotional connection that is essential for relationship satisfaction.

Breaking Stereotypes In The Kitchen

The kitchen has long been perceived as a space governed by gender roles and expectations. For centuries, society has assigned cooking to women, often relegating men to the roles of farmers, hunters, and professional chefs, rather than domestic cooks. These stereotypes have shaped not only how food is prepared and who prepares it but also how cooking is valued and seen in different cultures. Over time, however, societal views on gender roles in the kitchen have evolved. The breaking of these stereotypes is a reflection of broader movements for gender equality, the rise of culinary culture, and the growing recognition of men as capable and talented chefs, both professionally and domestically. This chapter delves into how traditional gender norms related to cooking are being challenged, while also highlighting male chefs and home cooks who inspire change and redefine the kitchen's boundaries.

Challenging Traditional Gender Norms Related to Cooking

For much of history, cooking was seen as women's work. In most societies, it was women who bore the responsibility for the kitchen, with cooking regarded as part of their domestic duties. From the perspective of traditional gender roles, men were expected to work outside the home, engage in physically demanding tasks like farming or hunting, and have professional careers. Cooking, especially within the home, was something that was thought to come naturally to women, rooted in motherhood, nurturing, and homemaking. Even today, some people still associate cooking with women, especially when it comes to domestic cooking.

The Rise of Gender Roles in Professional Kitchens

In contrast to domestic cooking, the professional kitchen has long been a male-dominated environment, particularly at the highest levels. The rise of the French culinary system in the 17th and 18th centuries, with iconic chefs like Auguste Escoffier and Marie-Antoine Carême, solidified the idea that cooking professionally was a task for men. At this time, professional kitchens were viewed as military-style institutions, with strict hierarchies and male chefs commanding respect for their culinary expertise. Cooking was seen as a serious, skill-driven profession that required expertise, which was typically reserved for men.

On the other hand, the domestic kitchen has been historically regarded as a space for women—less prestigious, often unseen, and less valued despite its critical role in society. This dichotomy became so deeply ingrained that women who worked as professional chefs were often marginalized or faced prejudice from both the public and their male counterparts. They were seen as exceptions to the rule, not fully accepted in the prestigious culinary world dominated by men.

Revising Public Perceptions: The Modern Shift

Over the past few decades, public perceptions of gender roles in cooking have undergone significant change, largely driven by societal movements advocating for gender equality and women's rights. As women began to enter higher levels of education and professional careers, they challenged the notion that the kitchen was exclusively a woman's domain. Feminist movements and campaigns for workplace equality pushed back against the gendered expectations that confined cooking to women's work in both the domestic and professional arenas.

Meanwhile, men began to challenge the stereotype that cooking was a task reserved only for women. This shift has been seen in various forms, from men increasingly participating in domestic cooking to a rise in male home cooks and male chefs who challenge the traditional culinary hierarchy. Men began to embrace cooking as both a profession and a hobby, and the rise of "food culture," especially with the advent of cooking shows and food media, has created a space for male chefs to gain widespread popularity.

Social media and television cooking shows, in particular, have played a critical role in challenging these gender norms. The rise of male chefs who are household names, such as Gordon Ramsay, Jamie Oliver, and Anthony Bourdain, helped reshape the image of the kitchen and cooking. But even more significantly, a growing number of men began to take up cooking at home, signaling a shift in perceptions of domesticity. Male home cooks now occupy a more prominent place in culinary culture, moving beyond the stereotypical image of a woman in the kitchen.

The Impact of Male Chefs in Professional Kitchens

The visibility of male chefs in professional kitchens has also played an essential role in breaking gender stereotypes in the culinary world. Male chefs, once considered the norm in the industry, are now increasingly seen as leaders of culinary innovation and mentorship. However, despite their prominence, women continue to face barriers in climbing the ranks of fine dining and professional kitchens. But there is a growing recognition of the importance of gender equality in the industry, leading to a push for female empowerment in professional kitchens.

As societal norms change, male chefs and home cooks alike have become champions of a more inclusive kitchen, where both men and women can find a place based on their skills, passion, and creativity, rather than their gender.

Profiles of Male Chefs and Home Cooks Who Inspire Change

Throughout history, there have been male chefs who have influenced both professional cooking and how the broader public perceives the role of men in the kitchen. Their work has helped to create a more inclusive space for cooking, breaking down the boundaries that historically separated male and female culinary roles.

1. Gordon Ramsay: The Celebrity Chef Who Redefines Kitchen Authority

Gordon Ramsay is perhaps one of the most famous chefs in the world, known not only for his Michelin stars but also for his fiery temper and commanding presence on television. However, Ramsay's influence extends beyond his professional accomplishments. He has been instrumental in reshaping the idea of what it means to be a male chef in the modern era. With his various television programs, such as *Hell's Kitchen* and *MasterChef*, Ramsay has popularized the image of the celebrity chef, elevating the profession to new heights. His approachable persona in the kitchen challenges the notion that cooking is an exclusively female endeavor, and he encourages both men and women to take ownership of their cooking skills.

Ramsay has also used his platform to promote diversity and equality within the culinary world, often championing women chefs and encouraging them to take leadership roles. His example shows that cooking is not just a profession for women to care for their families—it can also be a space for men to thrive creatively and professionally.

2. Jamie Oliver: Cooking for the Home

Jamie Oliver is another influential male figure who has brought the kitchen into the homes of millions, especially through his focus on easy-to-make, health-conscious meals. Oliver's approach to cooking challenges the traditional view that the kitchen is a woman's space by making cooking accessible and fun for all. He encourages families to cook together, and his philosophy revolves around the idea that food should be simple, delicious, and unpretentious.

His campaigns, such as the *Food Revolution*, aim to improve school lunches, raise awareness about nutrition, and bring people back to the kitchen. By making cooking a family activity, Oliver fosters a more inclusive approach where both men and women share the responsibility of meal preparation. His ability to connect with audiences has made him a role model for men who want to cook at home and in a way that promotes health and enjoyment.

3. Anthony Bourdain: The Culinary Storyteller

Anthony Bourdain was not only a chef but a culinary storyteller who brought the art of cooking and eating to millions around the world. His television series *Parts Unknown* showcased how food could transcend cultural and geographical boundaries. Bourdain's openness about his career in the culinary industry and his struggles with mental health created a space where male chefs could embrace vulnerability while still excelling in their craft.

Bourdain broke the stereotype that male chefs had to be overly aggressive or domineering in the kitchen. His approach was thoughtful and reflective, emphasizing the emotional and human side of cooking. By highlighting the importance of empathy, collaboration, and global connection through food, Bourdain challenged the traditional views of masculinity in the kitchen and brought forth a new era of male chefs who were open to breaking boundaries, both culinary and cultural.

4. José Andrés: Culinary Activism and Humanitarian Efforts

José Andrés, a renowned Spanish-American chef, is known for his innovative cuisine and humanitarian work. His restaurant empire, *ThinkFoodGroup*, includes concepts that emphasize sustainability and food equity. Andrés's work challenges gender stereotypes by showing how chefs, particularly male chefs, can use their platform to not only entertain but also make a social impact.

Andrés became widely recognized for his relief efforts following natural disasters, including his initiative *World Central Kitchen*, which provided meals to communities affected by disasters such as hurricanes in Puerto Rico and the Bahamas. His willingness to take a stand for what he believes in, both through food and his public actions, illustrates that cooking can be a powerful tool for change and social responsibility, one that transcends traditional gender expectations.

5. Male Home Cooks: Rediscovering Domestic Cooking

Male home cooks are increasingly challenging the gendered perception of cooking as a domestic chore for women. Social media platforms like Instagram, TikTok, and YouTube have allowed everyday men to share their cooking skills, recipes, and experiences with a global audience. Home cooks like *David Chang*, *The Korean Vegan* (Joanne Molinaro), and *Adam Ragusea* have become viral sensations by bringing home cooking into public view.

These male home cooks challenge the traditional view that the kitchen is solely a woman's space by showing that cooking is not just a necessary household task but an enjoyable, creative endeavor that everyone—regardless of gender—can partake in. Their presence on social media platforms has helped to normalize the image of men cooking in their homes, providing a much-needed counterpoint to traditional gendered expectations.

Conclusion
Redefining the Kitchen for All Genders

Breaking stereotypes in the kitchen is about more than just gender equality—it's about recognizing the universal nature of cooking and how it brings people together, regardless of gender. By challenging traditional gender norms related to cooking, male chefs and home cooks alike are inspiring a cultural shift. From Gordon Ramsay's televised kitchens to José Andrés's global humanitarian efforts, these men are demonstrating that cooking is not a space defined by gender but by creativity, collaboration, and care. As we continue to see more men involved in domestic cooking and women ascending the ranks of professional kitchens, the kitchen becomes a place where both genders can thrive, free from outdated stereotypes and full of possibility.

CHAPTER 6

Cooking as a Love Language

Throughout human history, cooking has transcended the basic necessity of survival, becoming an art form, a cultural practice, and most significantly, a powerful way to express love and affection. The act of preparing a meal is inherently tied to care, patience, and attention to detail, all qualities that are essential to building and nurturing relationships. Cooking, therefore, serves as a love language, where the act of preparing and sharing food is a profound expression of emotional attachment. This chapter explores how cooking is interpreted as an act of love and care, and how different cultures use food to convey affection and strengthen emotional bonds.

Interpreting Acts of Cooking as Expressions of Love and Care

Food as a Symbol of Nurturing and Affection

From the moment a person begins to prepare a meal for someone else, the act is infused with a sense of purpose and care. Unlike many other forms of affection that can be expressed verbally, cooking involves tangible, physical labor that requires time, effort, and attention to detail. When one person cooks for another, it's an expression of nurturing—of wanting to provide not only for their physical needs but also for their emotional well-being.

In many relationships, whether romantic or familial, food becomes one of the primary ways to show love. The emotional investment in cooking is deepened by the preparation itself: the choice of ingredients, the thoughtful design of the meal, and the presentation. Every step of the process, from choosing a recipe to laying the table, carries meaning. For example, preparing a favorite meal for someone during a difficult time or making their favorite comfort food as a surprise can show care in a way that words might not fully capture. It's a gesture that speaks volumes, offering not just nourishment but emotional support and connection.

Cooking for Someone as an Act of Selflessness

In romantic relationships, cooking can be a significant act of love because it often requires the cook to step outside their own preferences and desires in order to cater to the needs and tastes of the person they care about. The time and effort spent selecting ingredients, preparing the food, and ensuring it meets the preferences of the other person are acts of selflessness. It is an intimate gesture, where the act of cooking becomes more than just feeding someone, it's about putting another person's needs first, showing them that their happiness and comfort matter.

The psychological concept of "acts of service" in love languages, first introduced by Dr. Gary Chapman, highlights how some people express love through actions rather than words. Cooking falls squarely within this category for many people. The time and energy spent making a meal, especially a meal that requires effort or involves multiple steps, can show a level of care and affection that may be difficult to convey through other means. For many people, preparing food is a gesture of love that goes beyond satisfying hunger, but it is about taking care of someone, showing them, they are worth the effort.

The Ritual of Cooking Together: Bonding Through Shared Effort

The act of cooking together can also be a deeply bonding experience. Whether it's a couple making dinner after a long day or a family preparing a meal together, the shared effort of cooking fosters communication, collaboration, and intimacy. Cooking as a couple or family can build a sense of togetherness and mutual respect. In this context, cooking becomes an interactive experience, where both individuals or family members contribute and share in the creation of something nourishing.

The psychological benefits of shared experiences are well documented; when people engage in activities together, especially those that require collaboration, it strengthens emotional bonds. The act of preparing a meal together often involves synchronized efforts, from chopping vegetables to stirring a pot, which can mimic the harmonious teamwork that couples or families display in other areas of life. This collaborative effort fosters feelings of affection, companionship, and unity.

The Pleasure of Sharing a Meal: The Full Circle of Love

Once the meal is prepared, the act of sharing it is the culmination of love expressed through food. The experience of sitting down together, enjoying a meal, and engaging in conversation brings the act of cooking full circle. It's a celebration of not only the food but also the time, energy, and care invested in making it. For many, the shared experience of eating together reinforces the emotional bond between people, enhancing the sense of connection and care.

In romantic relationships, the act of sharing food often goes hand in hand with feelings of intimacy. Studies have shown that sharing a meal with someone can increase feelings of closeness and trust. This is because food is inherently linked to nourishment, and when shared, it conveys a sense of vulnerability; you're not only sharing physical sustenance but emotional nourishment as well. The experience of eating together is a fundamental way in which couples bond, express affection, and strengthen their connection.

Cultural Variations in Using Food to Convey Affection

Food as a Love Language Across Different Cultures

While cooking as an expression of love is universal, the way food is used to convey affection varies greatly across cultures. Each culture has its own set of food rituals and traditions that play a vital role in how love and care are communicated. Whether through the preparation of specific dishes or the practice of eating together, food acts as a bridge between individuals, families, and communities, offering a way to express emotion and strengthen bonds.

In Italian Culture: Sharing a Meal as a Family Affair

In Italian culture, food is central to family life, and meals are seen as an opportunity to nurture relationships. The tradition of the Italian Sunday family meal is a perfect example of how food is used to express love. In Italian homes, the preparation of a meal is often a family affair, with everyone contributing in some way. From making pasta to preparing sauces, every aspect of the meal involves cooperation and care. Sharing a meal together, especially on Sundays, is an expression of affection, a way of reconnecting and showing care for one another.

The concept of "cucina povera" (peasant cooking) is also significant in Italian culture. It refers to simple, humble meals made with love and care, often passed down through generations. The focus is on using locally sourced ingredients and creating meals that bring people together. In this context, cooking and sharing food is a means of preserving family traditions, expressing love, and honoring the bonds that tie people together.

In Japanese Culture: The Subtlety of Food as Affection

In Japan, food is often used as a subtle expression of care, and the preparation of meals can be seen as a way of nurturing relationships, especially in familial and romantic contexts. The Japanese concept of "omotenashi," which refers to the spirit of hospitality and selfless service, is closely tied to food. When preparing a meal for someone in Japan, there is an emphasis on creating dishes that are not only tasty but visually appealing. The aesthetic presentation of food, with its delicate balance of colors, shapes, and textures, reflects the care and attention to detail that goes into cooking.

In romantic relationships, the exchange of homemade food can be seen as a gesture of affection. For example, in the tradition of "bento" (boxed lunch), a partner might prepare a beautifully arranged meal for the other, often including foods that hold special meaning for the couple. These meals are often crafted with an understanding of the other person's preferences and desires, conveying affection through both the effort and the personal touches.

In Indian Culture: The Spiritual Connection Through Food

In India, food is often linked to spirituality and reverence. Preparing a meal for a loved one can be an act of devotion, both to the person and to the divine. In many Indian homes, meals are prepared with a sense of mindfulness, with great attention given to the flavors, textures, and balance of ingredients. Cooking is often seen as a spiritual practice, with the belief that food made with love and care nourishes not only the body but also the soul.

In Indian culture, food is frequently shared during festivals and celebrations, signifying the importance of communal bonding. The exchange of sweets, such as "mithai," during religious or family celebrations is a common practice that conveys goodwill and affection. The act of cooking and sharing food during these occasions becomes a means of reaffirming relationships and reinforcing emotional connections, especially within extended families.

In Middle Eastern Culture: The Role of Food in Hospitality

Middle Eastern cultures place a high value on hospitality, and food is central to the expression of warmth and care for guests. The sharing of food is a way of honoring and welcoming others into one's home. Traditional dishes like "kebabs," "hummus," and "falafel" are not only delicious but also represent the generosity and affection that the host feels for their guests. In Middle Eastern culture, the preparation of a meal for a guest is seen as an act of deep respect and love, where the food itself is a symbol of goodwill and hospitality.

In romantic relationships, food is often used to show affection. Cooking a special meal for a partner, especially one that is intricately prepared and rich in flavor, is a gesture that conveys love and devotion. The act of offering food in such a personal, intimate manner creates a bond that transcends the physical sustenance, reflecting a deep emotional connection.

Conclusion
Cooking as an Enduring Expression of Love

The act of cooking for someone is a timeless and universal way to express love, care, and affection. Whether it's a simple family meal, a carefully crafted dish prepared for a romantic partner, or a celebratory feast shared with friends and family, cooking conveys emotions that words alone cannot always express. Across different cultures, food plays a significant role in nurturing relationships, strengthening bonds, and expressing affection.

Through the act of cooking, we communicate our love in ways that are physical, emotional, and deeply personal. From the simplest of meals to the most elaborate feasts, food has the power to bring people together, to nurture the soul, and to strengthen the connections that make us feel loved and valued. Cooking as a love language is one that transcends cultural boundaries, serving as a universal means of expressing care and creating lasting memories of affection.

CHAPTER 7

The Social Dynamics of Women's Friendships and Food

Food has long been a central element in human socialization, and among women, cooking and dining are often more than just about nourishment; they are integral to creating, maintaining, and deepening friendships. The act of cooking together, sharing meals, and gathering around the table for communal dining offers a unique opportunity for connection, emotional support, and shared joy. For women, food becomes both a medium for expression and a shared experience that strengthens bonds. This chapter explores the role of cooking and dining in female bonding and socialization, highlighting how culinary experiences have helped foster long-lasting friendships and meaningful relationships.

Role of Cooking and Dining in Female Bonding and Socialization

Food as a Catalyst for Connection

Throughout history, women have gathered together in the kitchen and around the dining table for both practical and social purposes. The communal aspect of preparing and sharing food has long been associated with female bonding. In many cultures, women have been the primary caretakers of the home and the ones responsible for cooking meals. However, it is not just the act of cooking itself that is important; it's the shared experience of preparing and eating together that fosters deep emotional connections and a sense of belonging.

The kitchen has historically been the heart of the home, and for many women, it serves as a space for socialization, emotional exchange, and mutual support. Whether it's mothers and daughters cooking together, friends gathering for a dinner party, or sisters sharing the task of preparing a holiday feast, food brings women together in ways that transcend simple culinary technique. The act of preparing food together provides a platform for conversation, laughter, storytelling, and a sense of community.

In addition to being a space for socialization, cooking and dining together allow for the expression of care and nurturing. Preparing a meal for someone can convey affection, while eating together creates a sense of shared experience. These acts are often emotionally charged, as women share not only food but also personal stories, advice, and experiences. This mutual exchange strengthens their connections and fosters a sense of camaraderie that can deepen over time.

Shared Experiences and Emotional Support

Women's friendships are often built on shared experiences, and food-related activities such as cooking, baking, or enjoying meals together; offer many opportunities for these types of experiences. The kitchen and dining table serve as spaces for the exchange of advice, emotional support, and even healing. Meals shared during moments of joy, as well as those during times of hardship, can help women feel understood and supported.

The social dynamic of female friendships often involves a high level of emotional exchange. Cooking together fosters an environment where vulnerability is welcomed, and deep conversations can unfold naturally. Whether it's discussing personal challenges, offering advice, or simply enjoying each other's company in a relaxed atmosphere, the act of sharing food often provides a safe space for women to open up and build trust. For women who may not always have a formal platform to express their thoughts or concerns, cooking and dining together provide a natural avenue for this type of communication.

Additionally, cooking together can offer emotional comfort. A home-cooked meal made with care is often seen as a gesture of love and friendship. For many women, sharing a meal after a difficult day or during a challenging life moment can be a source of comfort and solidarity. Through cooking, women show each other that they are valued, respected, and cared for.

Breaking the Ice and Bonding Over Food

For women forming new friendships, cooking and dining can serve as a great way to break the ice and establish connections. Inviting someone to a dinner party or a potluck is often a less formal way to socialize than meeting in a public place. The shared task of cooking or the enjoyment of a meal in a relaxed environment allows individuals to let their guard down, build rapport, and develop a deeper understanding of one another.

In many cultures, inviting someone into one's home and cooking for them is seen as a gesture of goodwill and hospitality. For women, this act of kindness and sharing can lead to the formation of lasting friendships. The time spent together in the kitchen or around the dining table provides an opportunity to discover common interests, celebrate differences, and form a sense of shared community.

The Role of Food in Celebrating Milestones and Special Occasions

Food plays a central role in celebrations and milestones, and for many women, cooking, and dining together during these moments of joy can enhance the emotional significance of the occasion. Birthdays, anniversaries, baby showers, holidays, and other special events are often marked by the preparation and sharing of food. For women, these occasions provide a time to come together, reflect on shared experiences, and celebrate achievements and life's milestones.

Cooking together during these moments creates lasting memories. Whether it's baking a birthday cake for a close friend, preparing a celebratory dinner for a new job or relationship milestone, or sharing a meal during a holiday tradition, cooking becomes an important way to commemorate the occasion and solidify the bond between friends. These moments of celebration often become the foundation for deeper friendships, as women share in the joy of each other's successes and milestones.

Stories of Friendships Strengthened Over Shared Culinary Experiences

1. A Culinary Bond That Grew in College

Sophia and Emily met during their first year of college, both feeling somewhat overwhelmed by the transition to a new environment. They quickly became friends, but their bond truly strengthened one evening when they decided to cook dinner together in their dormitory kitchen. Neither of them had much experience cooking, but they both wanted to try their hand at making a homemade pasta dish. What started as a simple recipe quickly turned into a lively and fun-filled evening of trial and error. As they fumbled with flour, eggs, and the pasta machine, their laughter filled the room, and their friendship deepened through the shared experience.

The meal they prepared wasn't perfect; it was a little too salty, and the pasta wasn't as smooth as they'd hoped, but that evening marked the beginning of a lasting friendship. Over the years, cooking became their favorite way to bond. Whenever life got stressful or they needed a break from studying, they would gather in the kitchen to cook a meal together. The act of sharing food and working together in the kitchen became their way of reconnecting, and the emotional support they offered each other over countless meals only strengthened their friendship.

2. Cooking Through Loss and Celebration

Maria and Julie's friendship was solidified through food during both difficult and celebratory times. When Maria lost her father unexpectedly, Julie was there by her side, offering support and comfort. One of the things that Julie did to help Maria through the grieving process was to cook her favorite dishes. Julie would prepare soups, casseroles, and simple comfort foods that reminded Maria of home and family. These meals weren't just about nourishment—they were about showing Maria that she wasn't alone.

As the months passed, Maria began to heal, and the two friends found themselves in the kitchen together once more, this time preparing a celebratory dinner for Maria's birthday. The act of cooking together, sharing stories, and enjoying a meal became a therapeutic ritual for them. It was a way to mark the passage of time, reflect on the grief they had shared, and celebrate the milestones of recovery and personal growth.

The kitchen, for Maria and Julie, became a sacred space for both grieving and rejoicing. Their friendship was deeply strengthened through these shared culinary experiences, and food became an ongoing symbol of their love and support for each other. Every meal they shared was not just about eating—it was about nurturing their bond and creating a lasting connection that would withstand the challenges of life.

3. Sisterhood and Shared Recipes

For many women, cooking is a shared experience with family members, especially sisters. Lily and Rachel had always been close, but it wasn't until they started cooking together regularly that they truly began to bond in a meaningful way. They inherited a collection of their grandmother's recipes, each one carefully written on old index cards, and began cooking together every weekend. The kitchen became a place of ritual, where they recreated their grandmother's recipes, adding their own twists and making new memories.

Over time, their weekend cooking sessions evolved into a deeper connection. They found themselves sharing not just recipes but their dreams, fears, and aspirations. As they chopped vegetables, rolled dough, and seasoned sauces, they also opened up to each other about their personal lives. These shared moments in the kitchen became a space for vulnerability and trust.

The recipes they cooked together became a symbol of their sisterhood, each dish representing a shared memory or inside joke. Their bond, once simply familial, deepened into something richer and more complex, all thanks to the culinary experiences they shared. Cooking not only helped them preserve family traditions but also helped them grow closer as individuals, strengthening their emotional connection and reinforcing the foundation of their sisterhood.

Conclusion
The Power of Food in Women's Friendships

The kitchen and dining table are powerful spaces for women to bond, share experiences, and create lasting memories. Food, in this context, is more than just nourishment; it is a tool for connection, emotional support, and care. Cooking together and sharing meals allows women to express affection, offer comfort, and celebrate life's milestones. These shared culinary experiences are often the bedrock of lasting friendships, providing a foundation for trust, communication, and mutual respect.

Whether it's through the ritual of preparing a family recipe, celebrating a special occasion, or offering a comforting meal during a difficult time, food plays an integral role in shaping and nurturing women's relationships. These shared moments in the kitchen and around the dining table help women create deep, meaningful connections that last a lifetime, proving that food, indeed, is a language of love and friendship.

CHAPTER 8

Men's Culinary Competence and Relationship Longevity

Cooking is often seen as a shared responsibility in the modern household, with both partners contributing to the preparation and enjoyment of meals. Traditionally, the kitchen was considered a woman's domain, but over the last several decades, men have increasingly taken on cooking responsibilities, both in domestic settings and in professional kitchens. The question of whether a man's culinary competence can impact the success and longevity of a relationship is an interesting one. Is cooking ability simply a practical skill, or does it carry deeper emotional significance that can influence relationship dynamics? This chapter explores the correlation between a man's cooking skills and long-term relationship success, delving into how cooking can strengthen bonds, increase relationship satisfaction, and contribute to overall relationship longevity.

The Role of Cooking Analyzing Correlations Between a Man's Cooking Skills and Long-Term Relationship Success
In Modern Relationships

In contemporary relationships, the kitchen is no longer just the woman's domain. As gender roles in domestic settings have evolved, cooking has become a shared activity. More men are taking on the role of primary cook, whether due to cultural shifts, individual interest, or the practical need to divide household responsibilities more equally. In relationships where both partners share cooking duties, studies have shown that this distribution of labor often leads to greater satisfaction, cooperation, and mutual respect.

Cooking is not only a practical skill but also an emotional one. The act of preparing a meal for a partner is often imbued with affection, care, and thoughtfulness. When a man is skilled in cooking, he demonstrates his competence in an area that is central to daily life. His ability to provide nourishing, delicious meals can signal attentiveness to his partner's needs, as well as the willingness to invest time and energy into the relationship. Men who are competent in the kitchen may also be perceived as more attentive, responsible, and emotionally available, which can foster greater emotional intimacy and satisfaction within the relationship.

In addition, the shared experience of cooking can help couples work together as a team. This cooperative dynamism fosters communication, strengthens their emotional bond, and can help build resilience during times of stress. Cooking together allows partners to engage in a non-verbal form of connection that fosters cooperation, creativity, and problem-solving skills. Couples who regularly engage in cooking as a shared activity may feel more closely connected and emotionally supported, which is essential for long-term relationship success.

Psychological and Sociocultural Benefits of Men's Involvement in the Kitchen

A man's competence in cooking can also bring psychological benefits to a relationship. From a psychological standpoint, men who are skilled in cooking demonstrate a level of emotional maturity. Cooking requires patience, attention to detail, and a degree of nurturing; all of which are vital qualities in a healthy relationship. When a man is willing and able to prepare meals, it reflects his understanding of the importance of providing emotional and physical sustenance to his partner.

Additionally, a man's involvement in cooking can challenge traditional gender norms. In cultures where cooking has been predominantly seen as women's work, a man who takes on this responsibility can break down stereotypes and contribute to a more egalitarian relationship dynamic. This shared responsibility can prevent resentment from building over time, as both partners feel that the demands of daily life are being met equally.

Studies suggest that couples with an equitable division of labor, including cooking, are more likely to experience relationship satisfaction. When men actively contribute to meal preparation, it can reduce stress and promote a balanced partnership. The act of cooking together also encourages positive interactions and increases the likelihood of a stronger, more resilient relationship. It fosters an environment where both partners feel valued, respected, and heard.

Cooking as an Expression of Love and Care

One of the most powerful emotional aspects of cooking is its ability to convey love and care. A man who prepares a meal for his partner is not only offering food but is also giving time, energy, and thoughtfulness. This can be an expression of his affection, demonstrating that he is willing to go beyond basic duties to nourish and care for his partner.

Many women in relationships with men who are skilled cooks express how much they appreciate this gesture. It is not just about the food but about the effort and thoughtfulness that goes into it. Cooking allows men to show affection in ways that might not be possible through words alone. The nurturing element of cooking whether it's making their partner's favorite dish after a long day or preparing a special meal for a celebration, can reinforce feelings of love, security, and appreciation.

In a relationship, these gestures of care are important, as they contribute to the emotional well-being of both partners. When cooking becomes a form of expression, it deepens the emotional connection, helping both individuals feel loved, cherished, and validated in their relationship. The more these expressions of care are present, the more likely a relationship is to thrive over time.

Case Studies of Couples Where Cooking Plays a Pivotal Role

Case Study 1: Mark and Sarah – Strengthening Their Relationship Through Shared Cooking

Mark and Sarah, a couple in their mid-30s, began their relationship with a traditional division of labor. Sarah did most of the cooking, while Mark was primarily responsible for household repairs and managing finances. Over time, Sarah began to feel overwhelmed by the daily responsibilities of cooking, especially after the birth of their first child. Mark, sensing his partner's frustration, decided to take the initiative to improve their situation.

Mark enrolled in a weekend cooking class to learn the basics of preparing healthy, family-friendly meals. His goal was not only to ease Sarah's burden but also to provide a meaningful way to show his love and support. As he honed his skills, Mark began preparing dinner once a week, and soon, it became a regular part of their routine. The couple found that cooking together gave them a chance to bond in a new way. Their shared time in the kitchen allowed them to communicate more effectively, share new experiences, and work together as a team.

Over time, Mark's culinary competence deepened their relationship. Sarah appreciated the effort he put into cooking for their family and saw it as a reflection of his commitment to the partnership. Cooking together gave them a space to relax, talk about their day, and reconnect, which ultimately strengthened their emotional bond. For Sarah, Mark's cooking was more than just a practical gesture, it was a symbol of his love, thoughtfulness, and emotional availability. Their relationship flourished as a result of the shared time in the kitchen, and they both felt more balanced, supported, and fulfilled.

Case Study 2: James and Leah – Cooking as a Creative Expression

James and Leah met during their final year of university. They quickly bonded over their shared love of food and cooking. James, having grown up in a family where meals were a central part of the social dynamic, had always loved experimenting with flavors and cuisines. Leah, on the other hand, had not spent much time in the kitchen but was open to learning.

James took it upon himself to teach Leah how to cook, not as a chore, but as an enjoyable activity. The couple made cooking an integral part of their relationship, using it as an opportunity to explore new recipes, create together, and challenge each other. Cooking became their way of expressing creativity and playfulness, helping them build a deeper emotional connection. Whether they were trying a complicated French dish or preparing a simple homemade pizza, their time in the kitchen was filled with laughter, communication, and shared joy.

For Leah, the act of cooking with James was an intimate experience that allowed her to connect with him on a deeper level. As they worked together in the kitchen, they learned to understand each other's preferences, share responsibilities, and celebrate small victories (like mastering a difficult recipe). Cooking became a form of self-expression for both of them— James through his culinary creativity and Leah through her growing confidence in the kitchen.

The couple credits cooking as a major factor in their relationship's success. The process of learning together, building new skills, and enjoying each other's company has kept their bond strong. Today, they often host dinner parties for friends and family, showcasing their shared love for food. Cooking together has not only brought them closer but also helped them navigate challenges in their relationship with creativity and collaboration.

Case Study 3: David and Emily – Cooking and Conflict Resolution

David and Emily's relationship had been strong, but like many couples, they faced their share of challenges. After moving in together, they realized that managing household responsibilities, particularly cooking, had become a source of tension. Emily, who had previously done most of the cooking, began to feel resentful as she balanced work and domestic duties. David, on the other hand, was uncertain of how to contribute effectively in the kitchen, as he had never cooked regularly before.

Rather than allowing this issue to fester, David decided to address it head-on. He took cooking classes and began preparing meals once or twice a week. Emily, initially skeptical, soon realized that David's efforts were not just about alleviating her burden; they were a way for him to demonstrate his commitment to their partnership. As David became more competent in the kitchen, the couple began to bond over shared meal preparation, using it as a space for open communication and conflict resolution.

Cooking together provided a platform for David and Emily to express their feelings, frustrations, and desires in a non-confrontational way. The act of preparing food became a tool for collaboration and problem-solving, helping them work through their differences. The time spent cooking allowed them to reconnect emotionally and communicate in ways they hadn't before. Their relationship grew stronger as they learned to share the responsibilities of both the kitchen and the home, reinforcing the idea that a partnership is built on mutual respect, effort, and teamwork.

Conclusion
The Impact of Cooking on Relationship Longevity

The role of a man's culinary competence in relationship success is multifaceted. Cooking in a relationship is about more than just preparing meals; it is a form of care, expression, and connection. When men take on cooking responsibilities, it can foster a sense of equality, enhance emotional intimacy, and contribute to overall relationship satisfaction. Whether through shared cooking experiences, the expression of love, or the creation of collaborative spaces for problem-solving, cooking has the potential to strengthen the emotional bond between partners.

As these case studies demonstrate, cooking is not merely a practical skill; it is a powerful tool for building and maintaining long-term relationships. A man who is competent in the kitchen brings more than just culinary expertise to the table, he brings emotional intelligence, empathy, and a willingness to invest in the partnership. Through cooking, couples can enhance communication, create lasting memories, and build the foundation for a successful, fulfilling relationship that can stand the test of time.

CHAPTER 9

Cooking Competitions and Relationship Growth

Cooking, at its core, is often a shared activity that fosters bonding and strengthens relationships. However, adding an element of friendly competition to the mix can take the experience to a whole new level. Cooking competitions, whether lighthearted or more serious, offer couples a fun and engaging way to interact, test their skills, and create lasting memories. This chapter explores how friendly culinary challenges can enhance mutual respect, promote fun, and ultimately contribute to relationship growth. By examining real-life examples of couples who bond over cooking contests, we'll see how a little bit of competition can go a long way in deepening emotional connections.

Exploring How Friendly Culinary Challenges Can Enhance Mutual Respect and Fun

Friendly Competition as a Tool for Strengthening Bonds

Friendly competition in the kitchen, whether through casual challenges or structured contests, can be an excellent way for couples to learn more about each other's personalities, communication styles, and problem-solving approaches. Cooking together typically involves collaboration, but introducing competition creates a new dynamic that can teach partners how to handle both teamwork and individual accomplishment. Engaging in cooking challenges fosters an environment where both partners must balance cooperation and independence, which can contribute to greater respect for each other's skills and capabilities.

When both individuals participate in a friendly competition, they are encouraged to push themselves out of their comfort zones, try new techniques, and perhaps take on roles they might not normally play in the kitchen. This shared experience allows for creative expression and often results in laughter, fun, and some lighthearted teasing. The spirit of competition can help couples bond by giving them a chance to laugh at their mistakes, celebrate successes, and support each other through the process. These experiences help reinforce a sense of shared identity and mutual respect, as couples recognize the value of each other's efforts, even when things don't go perfectly.

Building Trust and Teamwork

Cooking competitions, particularly those where the challenge is designed to be cooperative, can foster trust and teamwork. In a relationship, trust is often built through shared experiences where partners must rely on each other's strengths. Cooking challenges that require collaboration such as preparing a meal together within a time limit or executing a specific cuisine, can help partners practice coordination, delegation, and clear communication. Even if the competition is framed as a lighthearted rivalry, it encourages couples to function together as a team, which strengthens their ability to work through challenges in other aspects of their relationship.

Moreover, when couples engage in friendly culinary challenges, they have the opportunity to encourage and support each other. If one partner struggles or makes a mistake, the other can step in with guidance or a sense of humor, reinforcing a supportive and non-judgmental environment. This creates a dynamic where both individuals feel valued, respected, and confident in their partner's willingness to work through challenges together. These qualities—trust, support, and encouragement—are vital elements of healthy relationships, and cooking competitions provide an ideal environment to cultivate them.

Enhancing Fun and Playfulness

One of the most immediate benefits of incorporating cooking competitions into a relationship is the element of fun and playfulness it introduces. Food, by its very nature, is something that can be enjoyed in both serious and lighthearted ways, and the playful aspect of cooking competitions can deepen emotional connection by creating shared moments of joy. The stakes in a friendly culinary competition are often low, which allows couples to let their guard down and have fun with the process.

Whether it's a whimsical challenge to see who can make the best homemade pizza, a bake-off to create the most creative dessert, or a time-pressured contest to cook a dinner with a specific set of ingredients, cooking competitions add an extra layer of excitement to the everyday routine. These experiences become the moments couples can look back on and laugh about together, sharing stories and memories of how they both tried (and sometimes failed) to pull off a perfect dish. In these moments of fun, couples are able to see each other's lighthearted side and enjoy each other's company without the pressures of daily life.

Stimulating Creativity and Problem-Solving

Cooking competitions also serve as an excellent platform for stimulating creativity and problem-solving. Each challenge often requires participants to think outside the box, come up with new ideas, and adapt to the constraints or guidelines presented by the competition. Couples are encouraged to step away from their usual routines in the kitchen, whether it's sticking to a tried-and-true recipe or following the same cooking methods. This opportunity to experiment can enhance a couple's ability to work together creatively, as they must adapt to challenges in real-time and find new ways to overcome obstacles.

The process of coming up with a dish under pressure, while balancing both flavors and presentation, requires collaboration, communication, and a bit of improvisation. As couples tackle these creative hurdles together, they learn how to leverage each other's ideas and strengths, which reinforces their capacity for teamwork and innovation in other aspects of their relationship.

Examples of Couples Who Bond Over Cooking Contests

Case Study 1: Sophie and Michael – A Bake-Off Brings Laughter and Connection

Sophie and Michael, a couple in their early 30s, have been together for several years and enjoy spending time in the kitchen. While they typically enjoy cooking together, they decided to spice things up by holding a bake-off to see who could make the best chocolate cake. The challenge was simple but fun; each would bake a cake from scratch, and then they would invite friends to be the judges.

As the bake-off began, Michael quickly took the lead, deciding to make a more complex, multi-layered cake with a decadent chocolate ganache. Sophie, on the other hand, opted for a simpler, rustic cake with a focus on rich chocolate flavor. The competition was full of playful teasing as they both worked through their recipes, with each person trying to outdo the other with unique twists on their cake.

Despite some mishaps, Michael accidentally burning the edges of his ganache and Sophie forgetting to add sugar to her batter, both cakes were surprisingly delicious, and the couple found themselves laughing at their mistakes. The bake-off not only allowed them to showcase their skills but also helped them learn to navigate challenges together in a fun, low-pressure environment.

As it turned out, the friends who served as judges declared a tie between their cakes, and Sophie and Michael realized that the true value of the competition was not in who won, but in the quality, time spent together and the memories they created in the process. The bake-off reinforced their bond by providing an outlet for creativity, fun, and teamwork, and it became a regular tradition in their relationship, with new culinary challenges every few months.

Case Study 2: Claire and Aaron – Cooking Under Time Pressure

Claire and Aaron have been together for five years, and both share a passion for cooking. However, with busy work schedules, they found themselves falling into the routine of preparing quick and easy meals during the week. To inject some fun into their weekday routine, they decided to hold a "speed cook-off" once a week. The rules were simple: they would each cook a dish in under 30 minutes using whatever ingredients they had on hand.

At first, Claire and Aaron approached the competition with a lighthearted attitude, but as the weeks went on, the stakes got higher. They quickly found themselves pushing each other to be more creative and efficient with their time. Claire, who is typically more methodical in the kitchen, learned to adapt her approach to cooking under time pressure, while Aaron, who tends to experiment with new techniques, found himself having to streamline his ideas to make them more efficient.

The time pressure aspect of the competition brought out a competitive edge in both of them, but it also encouraged cooperation. They began to share tips and techniques, helping each other when one of them hit a roadblock. The weekly challenge became a way for them to bond over shared excitement and a mutual love of food, all while strengthening their teamwork and problem-solving abilities.

Through their weekly cooking contests, Claire and Aaron not only learned to improve their culinary skills but also enhanced their communication, support, and understanding of each other's strengths and weaknesses. Cooking became a way for them to reconnect after long workdays and further deepened the foundation of their relationship.

Case Study 3: James and Olivia – Creating Culinary Memories with Friends

James and Olivia, a couple in their late 20s, loved hosting dinner parties for their friends. They often found themselves battling for the title of "Best Dinner Host" by challenging each other with culinary tasks. During one dinner party, they decided to create a "mystery box" challenge. Each guest was asked to bring one ingredient, and James and Olivia would have to incorporate all of these ingredients into a meal.

The friendly competition brought out the best in both of them. James took charge of preparing the entrée, while Olivia focused on dessert. With unexpected ingredients like saffron, dried fruit, and miso paste in the mix, the couple was forced to think on their feet, creating a cohesive and flavorful meal under time pressure.

What made the experience even more memorable was the fact that they worked as a team, combining their individual strengths to create a meal that was well-received by their friends. The playful rivalry between them, combined with their shared goal of impressing their guests, made the evening even more enjoyable.

By the end of the night, their dinner was a huge success, and the experience became a staple in their relationship. The couple now regularly participates in cooking challenges, often inviting friends over to share in the fun. This ongoing tradition has helped James and Olivia create lasting memories, strengthen their bond, and enjoy their time together in a way that goes beyond the everyday routine.

Conclusion
The Role of Cooking Competitions in Relationship Growth

Friendly cooking challenges provide couples with an opportunity to deepen their connection through creativity, collaboration, and mutual respect. By introducing an element of fun and competition into their culinary routines, couples can enhance their communication, problem-solving, and teamwork skills. Whether it's a casual bake-off, a time-pressured cooking contest, or a more structured competition, cooking challenges can provide an avenue for laughter, support, and shared memories.

As these case studies illustrate, cooking competitions offer couples a chance to explore new aspects of their relationship, fostering a sense of playfulness and emotional intimacy. Through these culinary experiences, couples can strengthen their bonds, improve their relationship dynamics, and create meaningful traditions that will last for years to come. In the end, the act of cooking together—whether as a friendly competition or a collaborative effort, reinforces the importance of shared experiences and mutual support in the success and longevity of a relationship.

CHAPTER 10

The Impact of Cooking on Family Dynamics

I n many households, the kitchen has long been considered the heart of the home, where not just meals are prepared, but also where family relationships are nurtured, strengthened, and celebrated. Cooking has historically been seen as a responsibility primarily assigned to women, with men often seen as providers or distant figures in the domestic space. However, as gender roles evolve and family structures change, the impact of a man's involvement in the kitchen has begun to take on greater significance. His participation in cooking can influence family roles, redefine responsibilities, and create more balanced, egalitarian dynamics within the household. This chapter will explore how a man's involvement in the kitchen influences family roles and responsibilities, and the benefits for children who witness shared cooking duties.

How a Man's Involvement in the Kitchen Influences Family Roles and Responsibilities

Redefining Traditional Gender Roles in the Home

For generations, cooking has been considered primarily a woman's job in many cultures. In traditional households, the division of labor often placed women in the kitchen, while men took on the role of breadwinners. However, the evolving dynamics of modern family life, driven by gender equality movements, changing expectations, and economic necessity—

have prompted a reassessment of these roles. Today, men's involvement in cooking challenges these outdated stereotypes, offering a more balanced approach to domestic responsibilities.

When men take an active role in the kitchen, whether preparing meals for the family or assisting with daily meal planning, they contribute to a shift in family dynamics. The kitchen becomes a space for shared responsibility, where both partners—regardless of gender—contribute to the nourishment and well-being of the family. This redistribution of duties allows for a more equitable balance of tasks within the home, promoting a sense of partnership and mutual respect.

By stepping into the kitchen, men can contribute to the emotional and logistical aspects of family life. Preparing meals, setting the table, cleaning up afterward, and meal planning are all part of a well-functioning family structure. A man's willingness to engage in these tasks can lead to improved family functioning, reduced stress for his partner, and a more harmonious home environment. It also helps dismantle the rigid gender norms that have historically defined domestic work, providing both partners with more flexibility in how they approach family responsibilities.

Fostering Greater Cooperation and Teamwork

Cooking together as a couple or family encourages cooperation and teamwork. Men who take an active role in the kitchen provide their partners with a sense of support and camaraderie. Rather than expecting one partner to take on the entire burden of meal preparation, the shared responsibility allows both individuals to collaborate and divide tasks based on preference, time, and ability. In turn, this creates an environment where both partners feel equally valued and involved in the running of the household.

The benefits of this cooperation extend beyond the kitchen. The act of cooking together provides couples with an opportunity to practice communication and problem-solving skills, which are vital to successful relationships. Involving men in cooking and other household tasks can also lead to a more collaborative dynamic in other aspects of family life, from managing finances to decision-making. When both partners share equally in the duties of home life, it creates a sense of teamwork that strengthens their relationship and contributes to a healthier, more balanced family environment.

Challenging the Provider vs. Caregiver Dichotomy

Historically, men have been expected to provide financially, while women have been tasked with managing the home and caregiving responsibilities. By engaging in cooking and other domestic tasks, men challenge the rigid roles associated with being a "provider" or "caregiver." This broadens the scope of what it means to be an active participant in family life, showing that men can be both providers and nurturers.

When fathers cook, they provide their children with a more holistic understanding of gender roles, where caregiving and cooking are not relegated to one parent. This shift can break down stereotypes and create an atmosphere of equality within the home, where everyone contributes to the well-being of the family, regardless of gender. Furthermore, when children witness their fathers cooking, it encourages them to adopt more balanced and open-minded perspectives about domestic responsibilities, promoting an environment where both parents are seen as capable of fulfilling diverse roles.

Benefits for Children Witnessing Shared Cooking Duties

Modeling Healthy Relationships and Gender Equality

Children raised in households where both parents share cooking responsibilities are more likely to adopt progressive views on gender equality. When children see their fathers actively participating in the kitchen, they learn that men can take on nurturing roles and contribute to family life in ways that go beyond traditional stereotypes. This model of shared responsibility not only strengthens family bonds but also instills values of equality and respect in the next generation.

Children who witness their fathers cooking and engaging in household tasks are also more likely to grow up with a more egalitarian perspective on relationships. They observe that both partners can contribute to the family's well-being and that no one person is solely responsible for the home. This fosters a healthy understanding of teamwork and mutual support, which they are more likely to carry with them into their own adult relationships.

Moreover, when fathers demonstrate care through actions such as cooking, they convey that love and care can be expressed through practical actions, not just through words. This can help children understand that emotional intelligence and nurturing are equally important for both men and women. These lessons, learned at home, can shape the way children approach their own relationships in the future.

Enhancing Emotional Bonds Between Fathers and Children

For fathers, cooking with their children is an excellent way to foster emotional bonds and create lasting memories. Whether it's preparing a simple dinner or baking cookies on the weekend, the kitchen provides a natural setting for quality time with children. Cooking together allows fathers to share their skills, knowledge, and traditions with their children, creating opportunities for learning and growth. It also provides a relaxed environment for open communication, as children are more likely to engage in conversations with their parents while involved in an activity like cooking.

For daughters, seeing their fathers in the kitchen provides a model of strong, supportive, and emotionally intelligent male figures. Fathers who take the time to cook with their children, particularly daughters, break down stereotypes about traditional gender roles and show that men can be caregivers and nurturers. Similarly, sons who cook with their fathers gain insight into the importance of caring for others and learn to value cooking as a skill and a form of love.

In families where fathers are active in the kitchen, children learn to appreciate the importance of food and the effort that goes into preparing a meal. This fosters a sense of gratitude and understanding, teaching children the value of both the process of cooking and the act of sharing meals together.

Teaching Responsibility and Life Skills

One of the most significant benefits of involving children in cooking alongside both parents is the opportunity to teach life skills that are essential for independence and responsibility. By participating in meal preparation, children learn valuable skills such as planning, budgeting, organizing, and time management. These skills are not only useful for personal development but also serve as essential tools for fostering independence and confidence.

For both boys and girls, cooking is a life skill that promotes self-sufficiency. When children are taught how to prepare their own meals, they are empowered to take care of themselves and contribute to family responsibilities. This can boost self-esteem and give them a sense of accomplishment. Additionally, children who learn these skills early in life are more likely to continue cooking and eating healthily as adults, leading to a positive impact on their long-term well-being.

Moreover, cooking together as a family encourages collaboration and shared responsibility. By assigning tasks and working together, children learn the value of teamwork and the importance of contributing to household tasks. This can help them develop a sense of pride in their work and an appreciation for the efforts of others.

Building Healthy Eating Habits

When fathers and mothers cook together, they have the opportunity to model healthy eating habits for their children. Cooking at home allows families to control the ingredients and ensure that meals are nutritious, balanced, and aligned with their dietary preferences. By involving children in the cooking process, parents can teach them about healthy food choices, the importance of balanced meals, and the benefits of preparing meals from scratch.

Fathers who cook for their children and involve them in the process help to foster a positive relationship with food. Children are more likely to develop healthy eating habits when they have a hands-on role in preparing their meals. Furthermore, involving children in cooking provides an opportunity to educate them about where food comes from and how it impacts their health. This knowledge can instill a lifelong appreciation for nutrition and healthy living.

Conclusion
The Transformative Impact of Cooking on Family Dynamics

The involvement of a man in the kitchen has a profound impact on family dynamics, reshaping traditional gender roles and promoting a more balanced, egalitarian approach to domestic responsibilities. By engaging in cooking, men contribute to the emotional and logistical aspects of family life, promoting teamwork, respect, and mutual support within the household. This shared responsibility not only enhances the quality of family interactions but also fosters a deeper connection between partners.

For children, witnessing their fathers cooking and sharing responsibilities in the kitchen provides valuable lessons about gender equality, emotional intelligence, and the importance of teamwork. Fathers who actively participate in cooking and meal preparation model positive behaviors that promote independence, collaboration, and healthy living. These lessons will stay with children as they grow and develop, shaping their approach to relationships, caregiving, and self-sufficiency.

In the end, cooking serves as more than just a means of sustenance; it is a transformative force that shapes family dynamics, encourages emotional connection, and strengthens the bonds between parents and children. By fostering a sense of shared responsibility and teaching essential life skills, cooking in the family kitchen plays a pivotal role in shaping the next generation's understanding of love, care, and cooperation.

CHAPTER 11

Culinary Skills and Self-Sufficiency

In today's fast-paced, convenience-oriented society, the art of cooking has often been relegated to quick fixes, takeout, and pre-packaged meals. Yet, cooking remains an essential life skill that offers more than just nourishment—it fosters self-reliance, boosts personal development, and has a significant impact on how one is perceived in both dating and friendships. The ability to prepare your own meals isn't just about creating delicious dishes; it's a form of self-sufficiency that empowers individuals, builds confidence, and enhances their overall quality of life. This chapter delves into the importance of self-reliance in cooking for personal development and explores how cultivating self-sufficient cooking habits can influence perceptions in dating and friendships.

The Importance of Self-Reliance in Cooking for Personal Development

Building Confidence and Independence

One of the most significant benefits of self-sufficient cooking is the sense of accomplishment and confidence it brings. Learning how to cook, starting from simple meals to more complex dishes, fosters a feeling of mastery. The skills acquired through cooking, from understanding ingredients and measurements to experimenting with flavors, help to boost self-esteem and promote a strong sense of independence.

In a world where many aspects of daily life are outsourced or simplified (e.g., relying on food delivery apps, packaged meals, or dining out), learning how to cook for yourself is an empowering experience. It signals self-reliance and the ability to take control of your well-being. Being able to prepare a meal from scratch, plan your weekly meals, and make nutritious decisions is a reflection of a person's ability to care for themselves and make informed choices. These actions are indicative of a person's maturity and sense of responsibility, qualities that are highly valued in personal development.

The act of cooking also teaches patience and perseverance. It's a process that often requires careful attention to detail, trial and error, and an openness to learning. The more you practice cooking, the more comfortable you become with it, leading to a growth in personal confidence. This increased confidence spills over into other areas of life, as people who are self-sufficient in the kitchen tend to have more control over their other life choices; whether in managing finances, pursuing career goals, or fostering relationships.

Health and Wellness Benefits

Self-sufficient cooking is closely tied to maintaining a healthy lifestyle. Being able to prepare your own meals allows for complete control over ingredients and nutritional content. By cooking at home, individuals can choose fresh, wholesome ingredients that promote good health, rather than relying on takeout, which is often laden with preservatives, unhealthy fats, and sodium.

Beyond the physical health benefits, cooking at home can also be a source of mental well-being. It offers a therapeutic break from the busyness of everyday life, encouraging mindfulness and focus. The act of chopping, stirring, and tasting food can be meditative, helping to reduce stress and anxiety. Cooking also provides an opportunity to experiment and be creative in the kitchen, fostering a sense of joy and fulfillment.

By taking responsibility for their own nutrition, individuals can also better understand their dietary needs and preferences. This awareness not only contributes to physical health but also reinforces a sense of agency and self-care. People who cook for themselves tend to develop healthier habits and attitudes toward food, which can positively impact their overall lifestyle and relationships.

Financial Responsibility and Sustainability

Cooking your own meals is also a practical skill that can significantly improve financial management. Eating out regularly or ordering takeout can quickly become a major expense, while cooking at home is often more cost-effective. By learning to shop for ingredients, plan meals, and prepare food in bulk, individuals can save money, reduce waste, and avoid overspending on pre-packaged or restaurant foods.

Self-sufficient cooking also encourages sustainability. By choosing to cook from scratch, individuals are more likely to be conscious of food waste, use locally sourced ingredients, and be mindful of the environmental impact of their food choices. This increased awareness of sustainability is a growing trend in modern cooking, and it reflects a deeper commitment to ethical and responsible living, another important element of personal development.

Improving Organizational and Time-Management Skills

One of the key aspects of becoming self-sufficient in cooking is the ability to manage time and organization. From grocery shopping to meal prep, cooking requires planning and efficient use of time. Self-sufficient cooks often create shopping lists, plan meals for the week, and organize their kitchen to maximize productivity. These skills carry over into other areas of life, such as work, study, and personal organization.

The discipline involved in cooking for oneself can be a direct reflection of one's ability to juggle responsibilities and make thoughtful decisions. People who take time to cook for themselves are often better at managing other aspects of their lives, such as budgeting, scheduling, and goal setting. This sense of organization and time management can foster a sense of control and structure, leading to improved personal development.

How Self-Sufficient Cooking Habits Affect Perceptions in Dating and Friendships

Impressing Potential Partners: Culinary Skills as an Indicator of Maturity

In the world of dating, self-sufficiency is often a key factor in determining compatibility and attractiveness. A person who is capable of preparing their own meals and maintaining a healthy lifestyle is often seen as responsible, independent, and emotionally mature. Cooking for a potential partner is an expression of care, effort, and thoughtfulness, which are highly valued traits in romantic relationships.

When dating, cooking for someone or sharing a meal you've prepared is a powerful way to show that you're invested in the relationship. It goes beyond simply providing food; it's about offering a piece of yourself. Preparing a meal requires time, attention, and creativity, qualities that are important in any relationship. The act of cooking can also serve as a form of courtship, where both partners share an intimate, personal experience over a delicious meal.

For men, in particular, who have historically been less involved in domestic cooking, showcasing culinary skills can be a unique and appealing way to stand out in the dating world. Women, for example, often appreciate a partner who is willing to take responsibility for cooking, as it signals not only competence but a willingness to engage in a collaborative and supportive relationship. It challenges the traditional gender expectations of meal preparation, which can be refreshing and exciting for those seeking modern, egalitarian partnerships.

Building Stronger Friendships: Culinary Bonding Experiences

In addition to romantic relationships, cooking also plays a vital role in building and strengthening friendships. Sharing food is a universal act of bonding, and when one friend takes the initiative to cook, it conveys care and a desire to contribute to the relationship. Cooking together with friends is a way to create lasting memories, foster deeper connections, and enjoy each other's company in a fun, low-pressure environment.

For those who regularly cook for themselves, it can also be a way to showcase personal skills and invite others into their world. A dinner party, potluck, or cooking competition can become a social event that reinforces friendships. It's a space where people share more than just food—they share experiences, laughs, and conversations, which help strengthen the emotional ties between individuals.

Moreover, cooking is often an excellent icebreaker in new friendships. It's a shared activity that brings people together, and when someone shows culinary competence, it can generate admiration and respect. The ability to prepare delicious meals creates a sense of respect, as it signals that a person is self-sufficient, resourceful, and thoughtful—traits that are universally appreciated in friendships.

Perceptions of Independence and Responsibility

Self-sufficiency in cooking also affects how an individual is perceived in terms of independence and responsibility. People who can cook for themselves are often seen as more independent and capable, as they are not reliant on others for their basic needs. This perception is particularly important in dating and friendships, as individuals are typically drawn to people who demonstrate self-reliance and personal responsibility.

In friendships, those who can cook for themselves are often seen as more balanced and self-sufficient. They are viewed as capable of taking care of their needs and not relying too heavily on others for support. This can be a desirable quality in both personal and professional relationships, as it shows maturity and the ability to manage one's life effectively. In romantic relationships, this independence can be especially appealing, as it signals that the individual is not only capable of taking care of themselves but is also able to contribute meaningfully to a relationship without being overly dependent.

Social Perception of Cooking as a Life Skill

As more people embrace self-sufficiency in cooking, the social perception of cooking as an essential life skill has grown. In dating and friendships, cooking is no longer seen as just a domestic chore, it is viewed as a valuable life skill that reflects independence, creativity, and a well-rounded personality. People who can cook are often admired for their ability to take care of themselves and their loved ones in ways that go beyond the traditional expectations of food preparation.

Cooking competence also speaks to a person's awareness of nutrition, culture, and sustainability. These attributes can positively impact how others perceive them in social settings. A person who prepares meals with consideration for health, ethical sourcing, or cultural diversity is likely to be seen as thoughtful, responsible, and conscientious, qualities that are highly attractive in both friendships and romantic relationships.

Conclusion
The Transformative Power of Culinary Self-Sufficiency

Self-sufficient cooking plays a central role in personal development by fostering independence, confidence, creativity, and emotional well-being. The ability to prepare one's own meals is a fundamental life skill that not only nourishes the body but also cultivates valuable life skills such as time management, budgeting, and problem-solving. As individuals become more self-reliant in the kitchen, they develop a sense of autonomy and control that positively impacts their overall quality of life.

In dating and friendships, cooking competence is a powerful indicator of maturity and responsibility. It shapes how others perceive an individual—whether as a potential partner or a valued friend—by demonstrating self-sufficiency, thoughtfulness, and the ability to care for oneself and others. Cooking, as both a practical skill and an expression of love, brings people closer, whether in romantic relationships, friendships, or family life.

Ultimately, culinary self-sufficiency enhances not only the individual's well-being but also the quality of their relationships. The act of cooking provides a platform for growth, connection, and self-expression, making it an indispensable skill for personal development and social bonding. Whether for practical reasons or the joy of shared experiences, self-sufficient cooking fosters independence, strengthens relationships, and enriches lives.

CHAPTER 12

Cooking Classes as a Social Avenue

Cooking has long been an activity that brings people together, whether in the family kitchen or at a communal dining table. However, cooking classes, particularly in today's socially connected world, have become an increasingly popular way for people to meet new people, develop new skills, and, for some, even find romantic or platonic connections. The social aspect of cooking classes is undeniable—participants come together, share an interest in food, and bond over the process of creating a meal. This chapter explores the opportunities cooking classes present for meeting potential partners and friends, as well as the success stories of relationships sparked in cooking classes.

Opportunities for Meeting Potential Partners and Friends Through Culinary Courses

A Common Interest in Food

One of the biggest draws of cooking classes is the shared passion for food. Whether it's a casual interest in improving culinary skills or a deep desire to learn the art of French pastry, cooking classes attract individuals who share a love of food and the culinary arts. For people who are looking to meet others with similar interests, cooking classes provide the perfect environment for creating new connections.

In a cooking class, participants are often put into smaller groups or pairs, which naturally fosters interaction. This setting provides an opportunity for meaningful conversation, as the task at hand—preparing food—encourages collaboration and communication. As partners or small groups work together to chop, stir, and cook, they are naturally engaging in conversation, which can lead to deeper connections.

For those seeking romance, cooking classes present an ideal space to interact with potential partners in a relaxed and enjoyable atmosphere. The focus is on food, and the social nature of the class takes the pressure off more traditional social settings where the goal is to simply "meet someone." Cooking classes allow for organic, fun, and natural interactions where participants can bond over a mutual appreciation for culinary arts. For individuals who may be hesitant or shy in other social contexts, the shared experience of cooking together often leads to more comfortable, easy interactions.

Building Friendships Over Shared Experiences

Cooking classes are not just for those seeking romantic connections; they are also an excellent avenue for building friendships. The shared experience of learning something new together—especially something as tactile and enjoyable as cooking—creates a bond among participants. Whether they're bonding over the challenge of mastering a tricky recipe or laughing at their culinary mistakes, cooking classes foster a sense of camaraderie and mutual support.

For people who are new to an area or looking to expand their social circles, cooking classes offer an easy and enjoyable way to meet like-minded individuals. The sense of community in a cooking class helps people feel more connected and less isolated. Additionally, since the class revolves around a shared activity, it serves as a great icebreaker, making it easier to strike up conversations with others who are equally interested in food.

Another appealing aspect of cooking classes is that they often attract a wide variety of people, from different backgrounds, ages, and skill levels. This diversity makes it easier to find common ground and form connections, whether they're based on a shared interest in food, travel, or a love of learning. Friendships forged in the kitchen can often extend beyond the class setting, with participants gathering outside of class to try new recipes or enjoy meals together.

Low-Pressure Social Environment

Unlike other social situations, such as networking events, parties, or speed-dating, cooking classes offer a low-pressure environment where people can interact in a more relaxed and natural way. The focus is on learning and enjoying the process of cooking, rather than solely on meeting new people. This less formal atmosphere helps alleviate the anxiety and expectations that often accompany traditional social interactions.

For singles, the fact that cooking is a communal activity helps ease potential nervousness about making small talk with strangers. Instead, the shared task of preparing food provides a clear focus for conversation, allowing for more meaningful and organic interactions. People are able to bond over shared experiences in a way that feels more natural and less contrived than more traditional dating settings.

The structured yet relaxed nature of cooking classes makes them an ideal venue for socializing. People can engage in lively conversation while learning new skills, all while enjoying a delicious meal at the end of the class. For many, this is the perfect environment to meet new people without the usual pressures associated with dating.

Success Stories of Relationships Sparked in Cooking Classes

1. Clara and Max: From Cooking Class Partners to Life Partners

Clara and Max met in a cooking class at a local culinary school. Both had signed up for the class to learn how to make Italian pasta from scratch. Initially, they were paired together for the evening's cooking tasks, which involved chopping vegetables, preparing the dough, and perfecting their sauce. Although they initially had some awkward moments—Max had no experience with cooking, and Clara was more comfortable in the kitchen—they quickly hit it off.

Their conversations flowed easily as they worked together to knead the dough, and by the time the class ended, they had shared not just a meal but plenty of laughs. After the class, Max asked Clara if she would like to continue experimenting with pasta recipes at his place. Over the next few months, the two saw each other regularly, cooking together at Max's apartment and sharing more meals. They discovered that their love for cooking complemented their growing affection for one another.

Years later, Clara and Max are married, and cooking remains a central part of their relationship. They often joke that they found their love while perfecting a ravioli recipe. The cooking class gave them not only the skills to make a delicious meal but also the foundation for a relationship built on shared passion and mutual respect.

2. Emily and Jacob: A Friendship Built in the Kitchen

Emily and Jacob first met in a cooking class that focused on making vegetarian meals. Both were interested in healthy eating, and their class was a perfect place to meet others with similar dietary values. Although they didn't initially expect to form a deep connection, they were quickly drawn to each other's enthusiasm for food and their shared values regarding health and sustainability.

Over the course of the class, Emily and Jacob often found themselves teaming up to prepare dishes and exchanging tips about the best local farmers' markets. The conversations came easily, and by the end of the class, they had made plans to meet up outside the class and try a new restaurant together. Their friendship blossomed as they bonded over shared experiences in the kitchen and a mutual love for food that extended beyond just the class.

Today, Emily and Jacob are still close friends, often cooking together and exchanging new recipes. What started as a simple cooking class grew into a deep, long-lasting friendship, proving that cooking can serve as an ideal foundation for platonic relationships.

3. Sarah and Liam: A Cooking Class Date That Turned Into Something More

Sarah and Liam were both skeptical about online dating, so when they met at a local cooking class, they were both looking for something different: an opportunity to meet someone in a low-pressure environment. Sarah had signed up for the class on a whim, wanting to learn how to cook Thai food, and Liam was simply looking for a fun evening out.

From the moment they paired up to prepare a stir-fry together, Sarah and Liam discovered that they had great chemistry. They laughed as they tried to perfect the sauce, shared tips about favorite foods, and found themselves bonding over their mutual love of international cuisines. By the end of the evening, they had exchanged numbers, and their shared cooking experience became the catalyst for many more dates and a growing connection.

Their relationship grew quickly, fueled by their shared passion for food and cooking. They began cooking together regularly at home, experimenting with new recipes, and trying their hand at creating elaborate dishes. The cooking class gave them the space to connect without the pressure of traditional dating, and the shared experience of cooking together provided a solid foundation for their relationship. Now, two years later, Sarah and Liam are planning their wedding, and cooking remains an essential part of their life together.

Conclusion
Cooking Classes as a Gateway to New Connections

Cooking classes have emerged as an increasingly popular social avenue for meeting potential partners and friends. By providing a relaxed, enjoyable environment focused on a shared love of food, these classes encourage natural interactions and create opportunities for meaningful connections. Whether it's through bonding over a cooking challenge, sharing a meal after class, or learning a new skill together, cooking classes offer an ideal setting for building relationships—romantic or platonic—that can last a lifetime.

As evidenced by the success stories of couples who met in cooking classes, the shared experience of preparing a meal together can be a powerful catalyst for connection. It provides a space where people can connect over their passion for food, break down social barriers, and form bonds based on mutual interests and shared experiences.

Ultimately, cooking classes offer much more than the chance to learn new culinary skills; they provide an opportunity for people to connect, form friendships, and perhaps even find love. The kitchen has always been a space for bringing people together, and when combined with the social and interactive nature of cooking classes, it becomes a powerful tool for creating meaningful relationships.

CHAPTER 13

The Sensory Appeal of Cooking

Cooking is not just a mechanical task or a necessity, it is an art form that engages the senses in profound ways. The aromas that waft through the kitchen, the vibrant colors of fresh ingredients, and the rich flavors that come together to create a dish are all integral to the experience of cooking and eating. These sensory experiences do more than simply enhance the enjoyment of food; they play a crucial role in stimulating attraction and emotional connection. This chapter explores how the aromas, visuals, and tastes involved in cooking stimulate attraction, and delves into the psychological effects of shared sensory experiences during meal preparation.

How the Aromas, Visuals, and Tastes Involved in Cooking Stimulate Attraction

Aromas: The Power of Scent in Creating Desire and Connection

Aromas have an undeniable power to trigger emotional responses and even influence attraction. The sense of smell is directly linked to the brain's limbic system, which is responsible for emotions, memory, and arousal. Because of this, the scent of food can evoke powerful feelings of warmth, comfort, and even intimacy.

When someone is cooking, the aromas that fill the kitchen serve as an invitation to engage with the experience. The scent of sizzling onions, roasting garlic, or baking bread can trigger feelings of comfort and security, as well as generate excitement and anticipation for the meal to come. These smells also have the ability to create a positive atmosphere, setting the stage for meaningful interactions. In romantic settings, the right combination of aromas can heighten attraction and foster a sense of intimacy. A couple cooking together might feel closer and more connected due to the sensual nature of shared aromas, which trigger emotional and physical responses.

Certain foods are also associated with heightened sensuality. For example, the rich, earthy aroma of truffles, the sweet fragrance of vanilla, or the spiciness of cinnamon and nutmeg are known to have aphrodisiac qualities. When cooked or baked, these ingredients have the ability to evoke a deeper sense of desire and pleasure, both from a culinary standpoint and in the context of a relationship. The act of sharing in these sensory experiences—whether it's the enticing aroma of a favorite dish or the aroma of a meal that was prepared with care, can create a profound bond between individuals, enhancing mutual attraction.

Visuals: The Role of Sight in Creating a Sensory Experience

The visual appeal of food is another key factor in how cooking stimulates attraction. Humans are naturally drawn to colorful, beautifully presented meals, as our sense of sight plays a significant role in how we perceive and experience food. The vibrant colors of fresh vegetables, the deep golden hue of a perfectly roasted piece of chicken, or the smooth textures of a well-prepared dessert all contribute to the sensory allure of a meal.

Cooking itself is an inherently creative process, and as individuals chop, stir, and assemble dishes, they are often creating something that is aesthetically pleasing to the eye. The way a dish is presented—whether it's an artful arrangement of ingredients on a plate or the visually stimulating layers of a complex dish, can make the experience of sharing a meal feel like an act of creativity, love, and care.

In romantic contexts, the act of cooking becomes a shared creative endeavor that allows both partners to appreciate the beauty of food and the work that goes into making it. The visual appeal of food can trigger a sense of satisfaction and pride, both in the preparation process and in the act of sharing the dish with someone else. When both partners enjoy the visual and sensory satisfaction of a meal, the attraction between them can deepen, as they appreciate not just the taste, but the time, effort, and artistry involved in the creation of the meal.

Moreover, food photography and presentation have become a central part of social media culture, which amplifies the visual appeal of food as an avenue for attraction. Sharing beautiful photos of dishes and showcasing one's culinary creations has become an attractive feature in online dating profiles and social interactions. The aesthetic qualities of food, whether through plating, garnishing, or the arrangement of ingredients, serve as a visual display of creativity, personality, and attentiveness, qualities that attract attention and admiration.

Tastes: The Deep Emotional Connection to Flavor

Taste is perhaps the most intimate of the sensory experiences involved in cooking. The combination of flavors—sweet, savory, bitter, salty, and umami—can evoke strong emotional responses, from nostalgia to pleasure to surprise. The experience of tasting food, especially when it is prepared with care and attention to detail, can trigger positive memories and feelings of emotional warmth. The flavors of a dish can serve as a direct link to a person's cultural background, family history, or personal experiences, all of which shape the way they experience food and their connection to others.

When cooking with a partner, the shared act of tasting and refining a dish offers a way to connect deeply. The act of tasting together—whether it's adjusting the seasoning, adding more spice, or savoring the dish once it's complete—can be an intimate and bonding experience. The exchange of compliments and feedback on the flavors of the meal creates a shared sense of accomplishment and enjoyment.

Furthermore, when preparing a meal for a partner, the act of carefully crafting a dish that pleases their taste buds demonstrates thoughtfulness, care, and attentiveness. The personal investment in creating a dish tailored to another person's preferences can deepen emotional connection, as it shows a deep level of understanding and consideration. Whether it's making their favorite meal or surprising them with a new recipe, the act of cooking with the goal of pleasing someone's palate is a powerful form of affection that stimulates both emotional and physical attraction.

The Role of Flavor in Developing Romance

The experience of eating a delicious meal together can also ignite a sense of romance. The enjoyment of flavors, coupled with the social experience of sharing food, can enhance the emotional connection between individuals. Dining together—especially when the meal is well-prepared—provides an opportunity to relax, communicate, and share a sense of satisfaction. The act of enjoying the fruits of a shared culinary effort creates a bond between partners, as they celebrate the joy of a meal well done.

Certain flavors, like chocolate or spicy foods, are often associated with heightened sensuality and attraction. For instance, the rich, sweet taste of chocolate is widely regarded as an aphrodisiac, while spicy foods—particularly those containing capsaicin—are thought to increase heart rate and stimulate a sense of excitement. These foods, when shared between romantic partners, can amplify the sense of attraction and desire, creating a shared sensory experience that fosters emotional and physical closeness.

Psychological Effects of Sensory Experiences Shared During Meal Preparation

Emotional Bonding Through Sensory Engagement

The psychological effects of shared sensory experiences during meal preparation are profound. Cooking together is an intimate activity that engages all the senses—sight, smell, taste, and touch—which can trigger emotional responses that deepen a couple's connection. When partners engage in the tactile process of chopping, stirring, and tasting, they are creating not only a meal but also an emotional experience that brings them closer. The act of cooking together, with its sensory richness, allows couples to share a unique moment in time where they are fully present with each other.

These sensory experiences provide a backdrop for positive emotional exchanges. Cooking with someone allows partners to laugh together, share frustrations, and collaborate in a creative endeavor. The pleasure derived from the sensory aspects of cooking fosters positive emotions and can lead to increased relationship satisfaction. The shared joy of savoring a well-prepared dish further reinforces emotional closeness and the feeling of accomplishment as a couple.

Creating Memorable Experiences

Sensory experiences in cooking also help create lasting memories. The aromas, visuals, and tastes of a meal are often tied to specific moments in time—special occasions, celebrations, or intimate gatherings. The smells of a meal cooking on a holiday, the colors of a birthday cake, or the taste of a favorite dish shared on a romantic evening can become cherished memories that are recalled with fondness in the future. These sensory triggers help anchor positive experiences in the mind, reinforcing the emotional bonds that were formed during the cooking process.

For example, the smell of a particular dish might remind someone of a special date or a milestone in their relationship. The taste of a favorite meal prepared for a loved one can evoke feelings of comfort, warmth, and love. These sensory associations provide a tangible way for couples to connect to their shared history, reinforcing their emotional attachment.

Strengthening Trust and Communication

As cooking together requires communication and coordination, the sensory aspects of the experience can help strengthen trust between partners. Whether discussing the right balance of flavors, agreeing on how long to cook a dish, or adjusting ingredients to suit each other's preferences, the act of communicating during the cooking process fosters trust and mutual respect. These exchanges, combined with the shared sensory experience of preparing and enjoying a meal, contribute to a deeper sense of connection and understanding.

The positive feelings elicited by the sensory appeal of cooking also create a space where couples can feel vulnerable, supported, and valued. The shared experience of creating something together—whether it's a simple meal or an elaborate feast—encourages a sense of teamwork and emotional cooperation, which strengthens the relationship over time.

Conclusion
The Sensory Appeal of Cooking as a Bonding Force

Cooking is a multisensory experience that engages the senses in a way that fosters connection, attraction, and emotional bonding. The aromas, visuals, and tastes involved in cooking stimulate attraction by creating positive sensory associations and providing opportunities for shared experiences. These sensory experiences enhance emotional connections and play a vital role in relationship growth, as cooking together provides a unique opportunity for partners to engage creatively, collaborate, and communicate.

The psychological effects of cooking—such as increased trust, enhanced communication, and the creation of lasting memories, further solidify the bond between partners. Cooking is not just about preparing food; it's about sharing moments that engage the senses and create lasting emotional connections. Whether it's the irresistible aroma of a favorite dish, the visual satisfaction of a beautifully plated meal, or the deep connection fostered through shared taste experiences, cooking provides a powerful and meaningful way to strengthen relationships and deepen emotional intimacy.

CHAPTER 14

Overcoming Kitchen Anxieties

ooking is often portrayed as an essential skill for everyday life, one that brings people together, nourishes the body, and offers an opportunity for creativity. Yet, for many men, the kitchen remains a space of uncertainty, fear, and insecurity. The idea of cooking a meal can feel overwhelming, particularly if they haven't been exposed to it as a regular part of their upbringing or socialization. Despite the growing cultural shift towards more balanced gender roles in the kitchen, many men still experience what can be described as "kitchen anxiety." This chapter explores the fears and insecurities men may have about cooking and offers practical steps to encourage confidence and comfort in the kitchen.

Addressing Fears and Insecurities Men May Have About Cooking

Cultural and Societal Expectations

For many men, the idea of cooking comes with societal baggage. Historically, cooking, especially domestic cooking, has been seen as a woman's task. Men have often been relegated to roles outside of the kitchen, either as breadwinners, hunters, or professional chefs, rather than home cooks. Even in modern times, some men feel a lingering pressure to conform to traditional gender roles, which can manifest as an insecurity about their cooking abilities. The fear of not "measuring up" to these ingrained expectations can lead to a sense of inadequacy or embarrassment when it comes to cooking at home.

Nicci Brochard & Dr.Ben Chuba

In addition to societal pressures, some men may also feel that they are expected to perform in the kitchen at a high level of proficiency, especially in the age of social media where cooking is often showcased as a polished and perfected craft. These unrealistic expectations can create self-doubt, leading some men to avoid cooking altogether. The fear of making mistakes, failing to follow a recipe perfectly, or producing something unappetizing can exacerbate these anxieties.

The Fear of Messing Up or Making Mistakes

A common insecurity for many men in the kitchen is the fear of failure. Cooking involves a combination of following instructions, managing timing, and dealing with ingredients that may not always behave as expected. For beginners, this can feel overwhelming, particularly when recipes call for precise measurements or specific techniques. The anxiety of not knowing how to handle certain ingredients or how to fix a dish gone wrong can cause hesitation and reluctance to step into the kitchen.

The fear of making mistakes is particularly paralyzing in the kitchen, as it involves the potential for disappointment; either wasting ingredients, not producing a desired outcome, or, in some cases, creating something inedible. The notion that cooking is a high-stakes activity that can result in failure makes it less enjoyable for some men, further feeding their kitchen anxiety.

Not Knowing Where to Start

For those who have not been introduced to cooking or have not spent much time in the kitchen, there is often an overwhelming sense of uncertainty about where to start. Men who have never cooked before may feel like they lack the foundational skills necessary to prepare a meal. This feeling of "starting from scratch" can lead to frustration or the belief that cooking is a complex, inaccessible activity only for those with experience or "natural talent."

With so many different cooking methods, tools, and ingredients, the sheer number of options can be intimidating. Not knowing how to use basic kitchen equipment or understanding how to choose the right ingredients can lead to feelings of confusion and hesitation, making the kitchen seem like an overwhelming space. As a result, many men may opt for convenience foods or takeout, avoiding the kitchen entirely rather than facing their insecurities head-on.

Encouraging Steps Toward Gaining Confidence in the Kitchen

Start Small and Keep It Simple

One of the most effective ways to overcome kitchen anxiety is to start with simple, easy-to-follow recipes. The idea is to begin with small, achievable goals that build cooking skills without overwhelming the individual. For instance, a beginner might start with a basic recipe like scrambled eggs, pasta with marinara sauce, or a stir-fry. These recipes require only a few ingredients and basic techniques but still yield satisfying results. The goal is to practice the fundamental skills, chopping, sautéing, boiling, and build confidence gradually.

When men experience success in creating simple meals, they begin to feel more comfortable in the kitchen. They learn that cooking doesn't have to be complicated, and their initial fears of "messing up" are alleviated by the small victories that come with preparing easy dishes. Over time, they can expand their repertoire, adding more complexity as their skills and confidence grow.

Embrace Mistakes as Part of the Process

One of the most important lessons to learn when overcoming kitchen anxiety is that making mistakes is part of the process. Cooking, like any other skill, requires trial and error. Even experienced chefs make mistakes and adjust recipes along the way. The key is to not let those mistakes define your abilities but to view them as opportunities for growth and learning.

For instance, if a dish doesn't turn out as expected—whether it's too salty, undercooked, or overcooked—it's not a reflection of personal failure but rather a chance to learn from the experience. Mistakes help build resilience and problem-solving skills, both in and out of the kitchen. If something goes wrong, take a step back, learn what went wrong, and try again. As confidence grows, so will the ability to troubleshoot and make adjustments on the fly.

Learn to Love the Process, Not Just the Result

Another way to overcome anxiety in the kitchen is to shift the focus from perfectionism to enjoyment of the process itself. Cooking can be a meditative and creative activity, where the emphasis is on the joy of learning and creating rather than on the end product. The act of preparing a meal is an opportunity to express creativity, explore new flavors, and experiment with different ingredients.

For many men, developing a love for cooking begins when they stop stressing over the "right" way to cook and instead embrace the fun and satisfying aspects of the process. As they learn new techniques and experiment with different ingredients, they can appreciate cooking as a form of self-expression and a way to care for themselves and others. Rather than focusing on producing a perfect dish, the goal becomes about having fun, exploring new culinary worlds, and enjoying the journey.

Engage in Cooking Classes or Online Tutorials

For men who feel particularly insecure about their skills, enrolling in a cooking class or watching online tutorials can be a great way to gain confidence. Cooking classes are designed for people at various skill levels, offering both practical advice and hands-on learning experiences. The structure and guidance provided by a class can ease the anxiety of figuring out what to do next and allow participants to learn from an expert in a supportive environment.

Online resources, such as YouTube cooking channels or food blogs, offer a wealth of tutorials that walk viewers through recipes step by step. These visual aids make it easy to follow along and see what the process should look like, reducing the intimidation factor. Some platforms also offer cooking challenges or themed lessons that provide a fun way to practice new skills while receiving feedback from other participants.

Practice Mindfulness in the Kitchen

Mindfulness techniques can also help alleviate kitchen anxieties. Practicing mindfulness in the kitchen involves staying present in the moment, focusing on the task at hand, and letting go of worries or distractions. By approaching cooking as a form of self-care and relaxation, men can reduce the stress associated with preparing meals.

For example, focusing on the sensory aspects of cooking, such as the feel of the knife as it slices through vegetables, the sound of ingredients sizzling in the pan, or the aroma of garlic sautéing can help create a calm, enjoyable cooking experience. Rather than rushing through the meal preparation, mindfulness encourages men to slow down, savor the process, and appreciate the simple joys of cooking.

Get Support from a Partner or Friend

For men who feel particularly anxious about cooking, getting support from a partner, friend, or family member can be a great way to build confidence. Cooking together allows for shared responsibility, which can ease the pressure. Having someone by your side to guide you, offer tips, or simply enjoy the experience with you can make cooking feel less intimidating and more enjoyable.

Additionally, cooking with someone else provides an opportunity to learn from each other and share cooking tips and tricks. The collaborative nature of cooking together fosters positive communication and reduces the anxiety of trying to get everything perfect on your own. Many people find that cooking together can become a bonding activity that not only improves cooking skills but also strengthens relationships.

Conclusion
Gaining Confidence in the Kitchen

Overcoming kitchen anxiety is a process that requires patience, practice, and a willingness to let go of perfectionism. For many men, the fear of cooking stems from societal pressures, a fear of failure, or a lack of experience. However, by starting small, embracing mistakes, learning to enjoy the process, and seeking guidance from classes or online resources, men can gain the confidence they need to enjoy cooking.

Self-sufficiency in cooking is not just about preparing meals; it's about empowering oneself, building confidence, and fostering creativity. By shifting the focus from perfection to enjoyment and learning, men can transform their relationship with the kitchen into one of excitement and fulfillment. Ultimately, the ability to cook with confidence is a life skill that enhances personal development, strengthens relationships, and opens up new opportunities for creativity, connection, and joy. The kitchen, once a place of anxiety, can become a space of confidence, satisfaction, and fulfillment.

CHAPTER 15

Embracing the Culinary Journey Together

Cooking is more than just an act of preparing food; it's a journey of discovery, creativity, and shared experience. When couples and friends embark on this culinary journey together, it opens up new avenues for bonding, communication, and mutual growth. From cooking a simple meal to experimenting with complex recipes or exploring cuisines from around the world, cooking offers endless opportunities for connection and adventure. This chapter delves into how couples and friends can embrace cooking as a shared adventure and the lasting connections it fosters. It also explores the enduring ties between love, friendship, and the culinary arts, and how they intertwine to create memorable experiences.

Encouraging Couples and Friends to Explore Cooking as a Shared Adventure

Cooking as a Shared Experience: More Than Just a Meal

At its core, cooking together as a couple or with friends is about more than simply preparing food. It's a collaborative experience where people engage with one another, exchange ideas, share laughter, and sometimes even face challenges together. Whether it's a date night in the kitchen, a family gathering, or a weekend with friends, cooking provides a unique space for shared creativity and fun.

For couples, cooking can be a way to explore and express their creativity together. It provides a shared goal and offers opportunities to work as a team, whether it's deciding what to cook, dividing tasks, or adapting the recipe to personal tastes. The act of collaborating in the kitchen can foster communication, enhance problem-solving skills, and help deepen emotional intimacy. Cooking together encourages teamwork, patience, and trust—qualities that are essential to healthy relationships.

For friends, cooking can become a memorable bonding experience. Sharing the task of preparing a meal allows friends to reconnect, try new things, and create something special together. Whether it's hosting a potluck, a themed dinner party, or a cooking competition, the kitchen becomes a space for shared adventure. Friends can experiment with different cuisines, cooking techniques, or dietary preferences, making it a fun and educational experience.

The Joy of Discovering New Cuisines and Techniques Together

One of the most exciting aspects of cooking as a shared adventure is the opportunity to explore new cuisines and cooking techniques. For couples and friends who love food, cooking together can become a journey of culinary discovery. Whether it's trying to recreate a favorite dish from a restaurant or venturing into uncharted culinary territory, the process of learning and experimenting together is part of the fun.

Cooking from different cultures offers a window into the traditions, flavors, and history of a place. A couple might find themselves making homemade sushi or exploring the art of Italian pasta-making. Friends could join forces to make a Mediterranean mezze spread or tackle the challenge of preparing French pastries. As they venture into new cuisines, they not only discover new tastes but also deepen their appreciation for the global tapestry of food.

The shared experience of cooking unfamiliar dishes also builds a sense of accomplishment and excitement. When a dish turns out perfectly or when it takes an unexpected turn, it becomes part of the adventure. These moments of trial and triumph are what make cooking together so rewarding. By stepping outside of their comfort zones and embracing the challenges of unfamiliar recipes, couples and friends can strengthen their bonds while experiencing the joy of culinary discovery.

Cooking as a Way to Connect Beyond the Kitchen

Cooking together isn't just about what happens in the kitchen—it can also set the tone for deeper conversations and meaningful connections. The kitchen, with its sights, sounds, and smells, is a space where people often feel more at ease and open to talking. For couples, cooking together creates a casual, non-pressured environment to communicate and share thoughts, feelings, and ideas. The act of cooking side by side allows for meaningful exchanges that might not happen in other settings. It's an opportunity to connect emotionally while focusing on something practical and rewarding.

For friends, cooking together creates a space for shared memories and storytelling. As they chop, stir, and taste, they can reminisce about old experiences, talk about their hopes and dreams, or share funny anecdotes. Cooking is often a perfect setting for bonding over shared experiences, deepening friendships, and building new memories that will last a lifetime.

Ultimately, cooking as a shared adventure fosters a sense of connection that goes beyond the meal itself. It allows for emotional closeness, mutual support, and the creation of lasting memories that go far beyond the flavors on the plate.

Final Thoughts on the Enduring Connection Between Love, Friendship, and the Culinary Arts

Food as the Heart of Connection

Food has always been central to human relationships. It brings people together, fosters communication, and creates a sense of shared experience. The connection between food and love is timeless; whether it's a grandmother making her signature dish for the family, a couple sharing a romantic dinner, or friends gathering around a meal. The act of preparing and sharing food has always been a way to show care, to nourish the body and soul, and to build emotional bonds.

In relationships, romantic or platonic, food serves as a way to demonstrate affection, express creativity, and foster connection. Cooking together as a couple or with friends allows for shared experiences that strengthen relationships, encourage cooperation, and build lasting memories. The kitchen becomes a space for emotional expression, where both the simple and complex tasks of cooking offer opportunities for teamwork, laughter, and love.

Moreover, cooking allows people to show appreciation and care in tangible ways. Preparing a favorite meal for a partner, cooking together to celebrate an occasion, or sharing a meal with friends all demonstrate love and thoughtfulness. It's not just the food itself, but the act of cooking, the time spent together, and the intention behind it that make these moments special.

The Power of Culinary Adventures in Building Lasting Relationships

The culinary journey is an ongoing adventure that evolves with time. Couples and friends can continue to explore new flavors, try new techniques, and create new dishes together, strengthening their relationships along the way. Cooking together is not just about the final product; it's about the shared experience of creation. It's about learning, growing, and enjoying the process of discovery together.

In romantic relationships, cooking together can become a metaphor for how partners approach life: with cooperation, flexibility, and shared goals. In friendships, cooking together creates opportunities for fun, laughter, and meaningful connection. Whether it's in the kitchen, around the dining table, or beyond, the experience of cooking and eating together provides a space for emotional expression, creativity, and shared adventure.

The Culinary Arts as a Celebration of Life

At its core, cooking is a celebration of life. It's an opportunity to express joy, creativity, and love through food. It allows people to connect with others, build relationships, and create lasting memories. Whether preparing a simple meal at home or embarking on an adventurous culinary journey, the act of cooking is an expression of care, nourishment, and connection.

In the grand scheme of love and friendship, cooking together is a powerful reminder that life is about the moments we share, the experiences we create, and the connections we foster. The kitchen becomes a space where people can grow closer, laugh together, and bond over shared meals. As we continue to explore the culinary journey together, we find that love and friendship are not only nurtured through shared moments of joy, but also through the act of creating, cooking, and eating together.

Final Reflection

Cooking is an art, a practice, and a language of connection. Whether as an adventure with a romantic partner or a shared activity among friends, cooking together fosters creativity, nurtures relationships, and creates unforgettable memories. The sensory experiences involved in preparing and sharing food deepen emotional bonds, while the act of cooking itself can serve as a metaphor for relationship growth: from experimentation and mistakes to success and satisfaction. As couples and friends explore the culinary world together, they embark on a shared adventure that nurtures not only their bodies but also their hearts. The kitchen, in its warmth and creativity, becomes a space where love, friendship, and life itself are celebrated through the art of cooking.

Conclusion

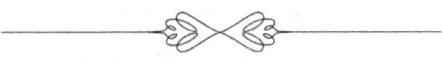

Culinary skills are more than just the ability to prepare food; they are a powerful tool for enhancing both romantic and platonic relationships. Throughout this journey, we have explored how cooking serves as an avenue for communication, creativity, and shared experience, and how these qualities translate into deeper emotional connections. Whether through the act of preparing a meal together, experimenting with new recipes, or simply enjoying the sensory experience of food, cooking has the potential to enrich relationships, foster intimacy, and create lasting memories.

One of the key reasons why culinary skills are so effective in enhancing relationships is their ability to bring people together. Cooking inherently involves collaboration and shared effort, whether it's partners working side by side in the kitchen or friends coming together to prepare a meal for a group. This shared experience fosters teamwork, mutual respect, and trust. In romantic relationships, cooking becomes a way to nurture each other, express care, and demonstrate affection. The act of preparing a meal for someone goes beyond just feeding them; it's a tangible expression of love, thoughtfulness, and emotional investment. Likewise, for friends, cooking together offers a platform for bonding over shared interests, creating new memories, and celebrating their connection.

Cooking also taps into the sensory aspects of connection—aromas, flavors, textures, and visuals—all of which heighten attraction and create positive emotional responses. The sight of a beautifully plated dish, the comforting aroma of a home-cooked meal, and the shared joy of tasting something delicious together create a sensory experience that strengthens emotional bonds. In romantic relationships, these sensory experiences serve as moments of closeness and intimacy, enhancing attraction and deepening affection. For friendships, shared cooking experiences create a space for enjoyment, laughter, and a sense of mutual appreciation, all of which contribute to the strengthening of those bonds.

Another compelling reason why culinary skills are important in relationships is their ability to foster self-sufficiency and personal growth. Learning to cook, experimenting with new techniques, and taking pride in the meals one prepares all contribute to an individual's sense of accomplishment and confidence. For men, in particular, developing culinary competence can challenge traditional gender roles and foster a more balanced partnership. Self-sufficient cooking also has practical benefits, such as encouraging healthier eating habits, saving money, and promoting a sense of independence and responsibility.

Cooking together offers a platform for communication, creative expression, and problem-solving. These shared experiences create space for couples and friends to open up, share their thoughts, and enjoy quality time without the pressures of daily life. The process of working together toward a common goal—whether it's preparing a simple dish or mastering a complex recipe—fosters emotional connection and creates opportunities for emotional intimacy. In this way, cooking becomes not just about food, but about building a deeper connection.

In conclusion, cooking is a multifaceted tool that enhances both romantic and platonic relationships. It is a vehicle for shared experience, emotional connection, and creative expression. By approaching cooking with openness and enthusiasm, couples and friends can use it to nurture their relationships, explore new dimensions of affection, and create lasting memories. Ultimately, cooking is not just about nourishing the body, but about nourishing the heart, mind, and spirit, making it a valuable and enduring tool for connection and affection in all forms of relationships.

Epilogue

The dance of love and nourishment calls us all; In that dance we find our truest connections. The men who understand this, who wield spatulas with the same care they offer embraces, have discovered a timeless secret. They know that cooking transcends mere sustenance; it becomes an act of love, attention, and presence.

As women, we recognize this language of care. We see in these culinary-minded partners a reflection of how we've long nurtured our own friendships over shared meals, whispered confessions, and the quiet understanding that to feed someone is to say: I see you. I value you. I choose to sustain you.

Perhaps that's the greatest lesson from our journey through kitchens and hearts alike: love, like the perfect dish, requires both boldness and patience, creativity and tradition, passion, and peace.

Bon appétit, to food and to love.

Nicci Brochard & Dr.Ben Chuba

Acknowledgement

Writing *Why Women Love Men Who Can Cook: Love Matters in the Kitchen and in Women's* **Friendships**, has been a deeply personal and transformative journey. This book would not have been possible without the support, patience, sacrifice, and inspiration of many people.

We are deeply grateful to the many hands and hearts that nourished this book during its creation. Like a complex recipe, this work emerged from countless contributions that transformed raw ideas into something worthy of sharing.

Our profound thanks to our editor Kamala, whose discerning palate caught flavors we had missed and whose gentle guidance helped this manuscript rise. Our agent Billy believed in this project when it was merely ingredients on a counter.

To the 34 couples who invited us into their kitchens and lives, sharing intimate stories of love expressed through food, your generosity flavored every page. The women's friendship circles who gathered around my table for those memorable focus group dinners, your laughter and insights were the essential seasonings.

Our family deserves special recognition for enduring countless experimental dishes and theoretical discussions about gender dynamics in culinary spaces.

Finally, to the readers who will bring their own experiences to these pages, may you find validation, challenge, and perhaps a

Nicci Brochard & Dr.Ben Chuba

new recipe for connection. Like the best meals, We hope this book creates space for both nourishment and conversation.

Thank you from the bottom of our hearts, and please consider leaving us a review.

Nicci & Ben